THE SAVVY
GLUTEN-FREE
SHOPPER

THE SAVVY GLUTEN-FREE SHOPPER:

How to Eat Healthy without Breaking the Bank

by

JENNIFER FUGO

Ignite Press, Philadelphia

Published by Ignite Press,
100 West Fornance Street, Norristown, PA 19401

Printed in the United States of America

Book cover & design by Ted Angel

Neither the publisher nor the author is prescribing nor treating any particular medical condition of the reader. This book is not intended as a substitute for the medical advice of physicians. The reader should regularly consult a physician in matters relating to his/her health and particularly with respect to any symptoms that may require diagnosis or medical attention.

While the author has made every effort to provide solutions to eating a gluten-free diet, the products and food the reader chooses to buy is entirely at their own discretion. The reader is responsible for verifying whether products and food they consume is gluten-free. Neither the author nor the publisher shall be liable or responsible for any loss or damage allegedly caused from the information in this book.

Neither the author nor the publisher has any control over and does not assume any responsibility for any changes in formulation or processing of any food products suggested in the book. Always consult a product's label and contact the company about its current gluten-free status before consuming.

To Nick, my Father and Mother, Dexter, Nicole and Chad for your constant belief and support in my vision and dream.

To Lisa, Uncle Joe, and Aunt Elaine for your words of wisdom and love that's always pushing me further.

To Grandmom Elsie and Great-Aunts Mary, Marge and Jean for your inspiration and passion for cooking and eating real food. Even though you are all gone, I feel like my work keeps me connected to you.

And to Michele Panoff and Heather Terry for helping me to conquer my fear of cooking and making it a fun, delicious experience.

"Time and health are two precious assets that we don't recognize and appreciate until they have been depleted."
— DENIS WAITLEY

TABLE OF CONTENTS

Preface...ix

Acknowledgements...xi

Ch 1. Gluten-Free Sticker Shock 1

Ch 2. Why is the Gluten-Free Diet So Expensive?.................. 8

Ch 3. How to Budget When Eating Gluten-Free 11

Ch 4. Stocking a Gluten-Free Pantry on a Budget 16

Ch 5. Food Storage Options and Tips.................................. 22

Ch 6. Vegetables 26

Ch 7. Meat, Seafood & Eggs 37

Ch 8. Legumes & Beans 41

Ch 9. Grains 50

Ch 10. Spices & Herbs.. 56

Ch 11. Fruit 59

Ch 12. Salad & Other Greens.. 62

Ch 13. Home Garden 64

Ch 14. Nuts, Seeds, Avocado & Coconut............................. 66

Ch 15. Helpful Kitchen Tools.. 70

Ch 16. Gluten-Free Meal Planning on a Budget................... 79

Ch 17. Gluten-Free Snacking on a Budget........................... 88

Ch 18. Final Thoughts 90

Ch 19. Gluten-Free Starter Recipes 92

Ch 20. Resources 123

PREFACE

You're not alone in feeling taken advantage of by food companies who see the multi-million dollar gluten-free food market as their next big boom. The more I learned about the gluten-free diet and how this "niche market" is bleeding us all dry while contributing to even more health concerns angers me. Not everyone is blessed with a good paying job and unlimited funds for food shopping.

You deserve to know the truth about why eating gluten-free seems so expensive as well as how you can outsmart the system. Before reading further, I want to share with you a couple of shocking points that are the foundation for why I decided to write this book.

Consider these two statistics for a moment:

1. The average American household of four **wastes 25 percent** of all food brought into the house. This can mean throwing away nearly $2,300 each year. [1]

2. Eating a gluten-free diet can be **242 percent more expensive** than a non-gluten-free diet. [2]

Shocking, yes?

You already pay a heck of a lot more to eat gluten-free and to then throw 25 percent of the money you've spent on that expensive food in the trash. Ouch!

Sure, you could opt for a tax credit if you've got a celiac diagnosis and lots of time to spare itemizing your grocery bills throughout the year. [3] But for the rest who lack a doctor's note confirming that a gluten-free diet is mandatory or anyone who has better things to do with their time, this isn't the most practical option, nor does it help you with that 25 percent of waste headed for the trash.

Though I'll certainly explain why gluten-free food can be more expensive, it's important for you to have these two points in your mind as you read through this book. They emphasize why the tips and tricks I will share with you are valuable and work. Plus, they allow you to start the process of becoming an educated and savvy consumer who has the mindset and initiative to outsmart the food companies (and organizations promoting them) that make a fortune off our issues with gluten.

So whether you are conscious of the total at the bottom of your grocery bill each week or you have all the money in the world to spare, this book will offer you practical insight to make the most out of your food investment without compromising your health. At the end of the day, that 25 percent food/money waste could turn into a vacation or some other opportunity for you and your family to enjoy life more. I have been able to do this along with many of my clients and now I want to share what I've figured out so that you can benefit, too!

1.) http://money.usnews.com/money/blogs/my-money/2013/04/02/how-much-food-does-the-average-american-waste
2.) http://www.ncbi.nlm.nih.gov/pubmed/18783640
3.) http://www.celiaccentral.org/shopping/tax-deduction-guide-for-gluten-free-products/

ACKNOWLEDGEMENTS

THIS BOOK IS NOT INTENDED to replace your doctor's or nutritionist's advice. Rather, it's an answer to a problem that the majority of people who need to eat gluten-free due to a health concern like Celiac Disease or Gluten Sensitivity– how to eat healthy and gluten-free without going broke. I'd like to take a moment to acknowledge the efforts of those who have helped support the creation of this book.

First, I want to thank Cristina Favreau for her persistent suggestion after learning this information that I should turn it into a book. Her assistance in researching and creating this book helped turn a lot of ideas into something everyone can learn from.

I am grateful for the editorial help from Kathryn Nulf who breathed life back into this project when it was stalled and shaped the message of the book to make it easier for readers to enjoy.

If it weren't for the daily assistance and guidance of Bryan Toder and Christina Daves, I'd not have had the platform and poise to share this information with the world. They are my friends who have selflessly given their wisdom and knowledge at all hours of the day. Early on in our friendship, they told me to write a book. I'm so glad that their words finally sunk in.

I'd also like to thank Karen Chiarini, Gracie Sassano, and Andrea Bracken who were my extra set of eyes. I deeply appreciate the time you each took to find details that I missed.

Lastly, I must thank my husband, Nick, who supported me through every phase of this book. Whether it was listening to me sort through my thoughts on material, being my cheering squad, or constantly allowing me the time and space to work on this project, Nick was critical to the creation of this book. Without his belief in me, I'm not sure this project would have come to fruition.

CHAPTER I

GLUTEN-FREE
STICKER SHOCK

THE WORST FEELING in the world is feeling like you're being penalized for eating gluten-free when in reality you have to for your health. With your diagnosis in hand, you know you must avoid gluten or else trouble will ensue. Your "trouble" might look different from mine, but at the end of the day, getting "glutened" just isn't worth it.

By avoiding gluten, you may have noticed a peculiar phenomenon at play—**it costs more** to eat gluten-free.

I'm probably not saying anything you don't know or haven't yet experienced. Whenever I ask our community what their biggest complaint of the gluten-free diet is, I'd estimate that 95 percent of people say it's the cost.

Case in point: I'm going to a friend's baby shower being hosted at a swanky restaurant in New York City. Upon visiting the restaurant's website, I learned that a gluten-free option is available...for **an additional $16**.

"$16?!?!?!?! Are you kidding me?"

The meal runs $60 for the "normal" patron, but now a gluten-free person is subjected to an additional $16. Ugh.

It annoys me (and many others in the gluten-free community) that some restaurants will now surcharge meals because I can't eat the bun. Or they'll leave a lonely hamburger on the plate, refuse to replace the bun, and then charge the same price for a fraction of the original meal.

When you go shopping, you have probably found that gluten-free products are often more expensive than their gluten-filled counterparts. Take pasta, for example. You can easily buy a one-pound box of whole wheat pasta for $1.29 (perhaps even less depending on the brand and where you live) while a bag of gluten-free pasta can run you up to nearly $5.00 per pound.

This is just one example of many where gluten-free products are, in many cases, grossly more expensive than what seems to make sense. Though there are some legitimate reasons for why gluten-free products cost more, there are also many instances where it's simply not fair to the consumers who need to eat a certain way for their health.

But there are ways to get around the sticker shock of eating gluten-free, and even buy groceries without breaking the bank. I personally know this because I had to figure it out due to life circumstances, and I've taught many clients how to do the same.

MY STORY

Before I go further, I'd like to share my story because I want you to know that I'm no different than you. I ended up in a situation where I had to figure out a solution or else it could spell trouble for my family.

In 2008, I was diagnosed with sensitivities to gluten, casein, eggs, and a laundry list of other items. Up until that moment, these foods were staple items in my life because I come from an Italian family. I literally asked, "What's gluten?" to my nutritionist as she gave me what simultaneously felt like a beacon of hope and a death sentence.

After getting over the initial shock and learning the ropes as best I could from the three websites I found online at the time, my diet changed. Fortunately at that time there were some semi-edible gluten-free foods in stores and online that didn't taste horrible. So I did the natural thing that many people learning they're gluten sensitive (or even celiac) do—I exchanged the gluten-filled options for those that were gluten-free.

To be clear, I honestly thought that whatever was labeled gluten-free was healthy. I'm not exactly sure how I came to believe this (and many out there still do), but I learned a serious lesson from eating this way. After a year of eating as many gluten-free brownies, cupcakes, cakes, and pastries—truly anything labeled gluten-free—that I could find, I was diagnosed with adrenal fatigue and candida.

On top of this, my husband lost his job. We didn't see it coming though we knew about layoffs at his company. His salary was two-thirds of our household income, and losing that was a huge hit to our ability to do and afford things (like the more expensive gluten-free food). Though he was able to file for unemployment and found a part-time job, his much smaller monthly stipend was nowhere near what we needed to maintain our pre-layoff lifestyle.

To make matters worse, a year later we came to learn suddenly that the state his company filed their taxes in did not pay unemployment benefits past a year.

For nearly three years following his layoff, my husband was virtually unemployed. He worked a handful of hours at a job that paid just above the minimum wage as he continued to search for other employment. Unfortunately, the industry he was in took a huge hit and only began to see a reemergence of jobs in late 2012.

This is why I am all too familiar with the struggles to put food on the table (gluten-free, no less) on a small income that for one year was not that far above the poverty line for a two-person household. We thankfully had some savings and were able to avoid spending most of that money because of my own tenacity and creativity.

When my husband eventually found a stable job again in his field, I remained committed to living gluten-free without breaking the bank. However, I was not willing to compromise my health in order to save money this time around. I now knew the consequences of eating cheap, highly processed gluten-free foods. At the end of the day, to save a buck or two at the grocery store was not worth it. So I decided to get savvy about what I bought and how I prepared and saved it.

MY PHILOSOPHY

Eating cheap is going to ruin your health. The demise of the health of America revolves around the rise of cheap, highly-processed food. Highly-processed gluten-free food is no different.

If you have not heard this before, allow me to spare you years of confusion: the "gluten-free" label does not necessarily mean that a product or item is "healthy." That is a pervasive lie that's been perpetuated by the media, celebrities, health professionals, food companies, and bloggers. Do yourself a favor and start to question every single product that has any claim attached to it in regard to healthfulness.

In the beginning stages of going gluten-free, it's okay to swap out your gluten-filled favorites for those that are gluten-free. But these foods should never be a part of your gluten-free diet long term, as it is for so many. This stage should be intended as a transition to get you going and off of gluten-based food.

Once you get the hang of eating and cooking gluten-free, then it's wise to begin slowly removing your reliance on those products and focusing your diet more so on whole foods. This simply means eating food that is as close to its natural state as humanly possible. An example of this is choosing brown rice instead of a hamburger bun made from rice flour. Ideally, you should focus on eating real food, so more meats, vegetables, fish, fruit, nuts, seeds, gluten-free grains, and legumes. Your diet can also include eggs and some dairy, if you can tolerate them.

And so I came up with this phrase which I share often—Eat healthy in a way that **happens** to be gluten-free.

The reason for this is simply to build and preserve your health. Processed gluten-free foods tend to be highly glycemic (meaning your blood sugar is spiking and crashing all day long), high in sugar (another problem for your blood sugar), loaded with toxic fats (which can be irritating to your already damaged gut), and filled with gross additives and ingredients that aren't good for your health.

They are also much more expensive, both at the moment of purchase as well as the cost of additional copays to doctors as you end up with more health problems just as I and so many others did. The testing that I had done was out-of-pocket in order for me to figure out all my issues, so it was more than just a copay to my local doctor. From both the short- and long-term perspectives, letting go of the gluten-free processed foods and switching to having more whole foods is budget-friendly.

And what makes eating real food even more budget-friendly is learning how to prepare, cook, and save food so you aren't wasting nor cooking every day. Creating plans dramatically increases your chances of eating well without breaking the bank. And that's where my expertise shines – in helping you find creative ways to take the hassle out of the cooking process and develop valuable habits that result in healthy, gluten-free "fast food". Not the type of "fast food" conventionally thought of with drive-thrus and dollar menus, but the type that require little effort and energy on your part so that delicious, healthy, gluten-free food is only moments away.

BECOME SAVVY

The tips I share in this book help us do just that—become **savvy**.

The word "savvy" is defined by the Merriam-Webster Dictionary as "practical understanding or knowledge of something" and having "practical know-how." People who are savvy are viewed as intelligent and wise. They make good decisions based on what they have available to them.

Price tag fixation is not the answer you're looking for when it comes to saving money. It's not about being cheap or eating gluten-free "on a shoestring." Those approaches to a gluten-free diet will get you nowhere, except eating cheap processed food and feeling lousy.

Instead, it's about eating well and becoming savvy by making good use of the resources (both money and food) that are available to you. This way you can know that you are making the best possible decisions to support your health. And it doesn't require that you compromise any part of what's important to you—namely, your health and your bank account.

At the end of the day, if you don't have your health, you have nothing. By being savvy, **you become an advocate for yourself**. When you take care of your own needs by eating well, you feel well as a result. It also allows you the ability to enjoy what is most important to you in your life because you have the personal and financial means to do so.

My process of becoming a savvy gluten-free eater isn't all that complicated or difficult. It doesn't require you to become a slave to your stove or to spend $200 each week to feed one person at the grocery store. Much of what you can do to lower your grocery bill while remaining efficient in the kitchen are completely common sense, but not always obvious. I'll share the exact steps that I teach my clients with you—steps that will, with some practice, become second-nature, just like riding a bike.

In this book, you will learn how to become savvy so that you can truly nourish yourself and your whole family. I will show you how preparing and storing food, changing up your meal planning routine, having the right kitchen gadgets on hand, and cooking delicious gluten-free recipes doesn't have to be stressful or costly. By incorporating my savvy tips, you will become more creative in the kitchen with meals and save money at the same time.

My intention for this book is to pass along the approach I adopted that has served me and others well during a time of hardship. I want to help you have more freedom to eat well without spending

$200 or more per week on groceries. Finally, I want to ignite a fire in you to become savvy and eat in a way that happens to be gluten-free so that meals are crowd pleasers.

CHAPTER 2

WHY IS THE GLUTEN-FREE DIET SO EXPENSIVE?

E ATING GLUTEN-FREE IS EXPENSIVE. There's no getting around it. Once you've read the statistics, it's clear that the squeeze you feel after every visit to the grocery store is not in your head. Eating gluten-free can elevate your grocery budget by **nearly 242 percent**! That increase can spell trouble for those with tighter budgets and prevent them from staying compliant. For others, it means you begin to give up vacations and other occasional experiences (like going out to eat with your family or friends). No matter where your financial situation falls, the spike in food costs can absolutely cause you to resent your gluten-free diet.

To avoid getting stuck in a negative relationship with food, let's break down the reasons why eating gluten-free is more expensive. I've found that knowing these reasons can help empower you as you learn the tips shared in this book. It will also explain why the focus is on eating less processed foods.

Here are the four main reasons why the gluten-free diet is expensive –

The first reason has nothing to do with a product being gluten-free or not. Pre-packaged foods, in general, are more expensive because you are paying for convenience. You are paying for someone else to do all the work for you—chopping, assembling, and mixing. That's the main factor right there.

The second reason gluten-free food can be so expensive is that gluten-free products usually have more ingredients in them than in traditional wheat products to make up for what's missing from gluten-free flours such as bulk and the ability to bind together. Therefore, they have to add binding agents like eggs, dairy, and various gums (e.g. xanthan gum) to give a similar consistency and texture as the traditional non-gluten-free items you are accustomed to.

The third reason is special processing, which means a separate gluten-free facility is required to avoid gluten cross-contamination. These facilities are more expensive to run. There are also certifications and testing that food companies will have to undergo to verify that the final food products you buy off the grocery shelf are indeed gluten-free. The expense of these additional safety measures are passed down to the consumer via the price tag.

The fourth reason why gluten-free products cost more is that, despite celebrities who talk about the wonders of the "gluten-free diet" and the mainstream media that cannot seem to help itself from constantly trying to undermine any part of the way we eat, it is still considered a niche market in the grand scheme of grocery items.

Your take-away message is that a diet heavily focused around gluten-free products is what will ultimately cost you more money. A boxed product has so many different "extra" costs inserted into the price tag that it is one of the biggest reasons for your sky-rocketing grocery bill.

And remember- products labeled as "gluten-free" do not mean they are healthy. I can't stress this point enough to clients and those within our community. A gluten-free brownie is still a brownie. A gluten-free doughnut is still a doughnut. You'd never believe someone if they told you that a wheat flour-based pastry was healthy… so don't believe that the gluten-free versions are either.

Now don't get me wrong—I'm not against all gluten-free products. I certainly do indulge periodically and there are companies out there that genuinely do care about the health-value and quality of their products. However, many gluten-free products are not healthy at all. Moderation is key. It's okay to have a gluten-free cookie or brownie as an occasional treat, but it's not something that should be part of your daily menu.

With this information in mind, you now have the foundation you'll need to make use of the tips I'll share in the proceeding chapters. Having the right mindset and understanding the reasons why things are the way they are can put you in the driver's seat. They also can ignite the motivation you need to begin integrating simple tweaks I'll share into your life that can save both your money and health.

CHAPTER 3

HOW TO BUDGET WHEN EATING GLUTEN-FREE

WHY BUDGET? Because no one likes throwing money away. When you realize that **up to 25 percent** of what you spend could literally end up in the trash, a certain sense of urgency takes shape around the conversation of budgeting your food intelligently. It doesn't have to be a consuming process that requires intense focus and time. Rather, savvy budgeting means that you "hack" your current approach to food and meal time.

To "hack" anything means to find creative, intelligent, savvy, more efficient, more cost-effective and many times easier ways to solve a given problem. Buying expensive gluten-free food (that's also healthy) is a problem that I've clearly described thus far in this book. I want to show you how to intelligently use the budget you have to go farther and afford more ease, comfort, and time in your life to enjoy what is most meaningful to you.

It's entirely possible to spend more time doing what's meaningful when you consider the specifics of what "hacking" your gluten-free diet means. Since 25 percent waste of gluten-free food could equal **upwards of $5500 a year**, it underscores why "hacking" your gluten-free diet to saving hard-earned money is important. Imagine what you could do with an additional $5500 each year? That could mean buying better quality food, going on vacation, saving for your child's college education, or enjoying weekly family dinners out at a nice restaurant. Or maybe it means having the ability to give up a second part-time job to "make ends meet" to spend more time with your spouse and kids.

By teaching my health and money-saving techniques to clients, I've had those who track their expenses say that these tips helped them lower their grocery bills by up to 50 percent! To get started, let's talk about the bigger themes that I'll expand upon in the proceeding chapters that will help you see results.

BECOME A PLANNER

In order to eat well, save money, and to wean yourself away from relying on convenient gluten-free products, planning is key. Setting aside just 20 minutes a week to plan meals will go a long way to saving you money.

To get yourself into a habit of planning your food for the week, determine when you could sit down and plot out what you want to eat for the week. Make this a permanent appointment on your weekly calendar so that you develop a sense of routine. Then decide which days of the week you'll cook (I suggest that you assume you're going to cook twice a week) and commit to cooking extra servings (or cooking in bulk) so that you'll have leftovers for lunch. Play with different ingredients to make meals interesting. I'll cover the process of meal planning more in depth in Chapter 16.

FIND TRUSTED GLUTEN-FREE PRODUCTS AT THE STORE

If you get anxious thinking about going to the grocery store, you may want to get your hands on **"The Essential Gluten-Free Grocery Guide"** from Triumph Dining. Look through this 500+ page book, find stores you locally have access to, and see what gluten-free options they carry. It lists tons of ingredients and foods, including frozen food companies and store brands.

You can also get a copy of the **"Gluten-Free Grocery Shopping Guide"** from Cecelia's Marketplace, which also is chock-full of incredible product information that will save you time once you know what's safe to buy at your local store. I have both of these books on hand. Familiarizing myself with the information based on where I shop and what I eat has been invaluable.

FREEZING FOOD

I can't stress enough to make good use of your freezer and pantry, and we will talk about how to properly store food in later chapters. Your freezer will become your best friend. Eventually, you'll know that what is in there is healthy and gluten-free because you made it. After a full day at work, you can pull something out, defrost it for 10 or 15 minutes, throw it in a pot or the microwave, add a few vegetables, and voilà! Not even 30 minutes after getting home, you'll have a home-cooked meal ready to eat.

SHOP AROUND

To save money, do not be afraid to look through circulars and shop specials, and compare store prices and weekly specials. When a store has a sale on gluten-free friendly frozen vegetables, stock up and fill your freezer. Frozen vegetables are much healthier than canned vegetables and adding them into meals is a great way to bulk up your dishes and add more veggies into your diet. Be smart about what you're buying. Purchase items in bulk when stores drop their prices. For example, there's a grocery store near me and their brand of frozen vegetables are sometimes a dollar a bag!

GET LOCAL

Check out local produce stores. Many times people hesitate going to specialty or produce stores because they are not sure what they'll find. Some have a lot of ethnic foods—Mexican, Italian, or Asian.

But most often, you can find great deals on vegetables and fruits. I go into one near me and I can walk out with a huge box of vegetables—enough to use AND freeze—for $20.

GO ONLINE

Check out online deals for non-perishables like flours, nuts, seeds, and other things that you can buy in bulk. Amazon.com is an incredible resource for this. Just make sure the food is processed in a gluten-free environment. You can't assume that something that might not naturally have gluten, like nuts, isn't processed on the same lines as something made with wheat.

A real-life example of this contamination issue happened when I was looking for dried cherries for a gluten-free cooking class I taught. I searched every single brand of dried cherries at Whole Foods and all of them were produced in facilities that had wheat. People with celiac disease can't take that chance. So when ordering online, always verify how the items are produced. If you have celiac disease, be sure to look for a dedicated gluten-free facility.

ORGANIC VS. NON-ORGANIC

What about buying organic? Some people don't care about buying organic and others simply cannot afford it. Some people can easily afford organic products and make it part of their personal mission to only buy organic. Other people prefer to buy local vegetables, fruit, and meat, organic or not. Generally speaking, if you are on a tight budget, going to a produce store is a great spot to save money on fresh and frozen produce.

"IS IT BETTER TO BUY ORGANIC OR NON-ORGANIC FOOD?"

I am often asked this question. My reply is simple:

- If you can afford organic food, buy organic food;
- If you can afford to buy just a few organic fruits and vegeta-

bles, refer to the Dirty Dozen Plus™ list for the best ones to buy organic;

- If you can't afford organic, buy the best quality you can afford and spend the bulk of your food budget on fresh vegetables.

Bottom line: There is no need to make this a complicated issue. Buy and eat lots of vegetables. Let your budget and your personal preference guide you to what's best.

If you have sensitivities to chemicals, buying organic is a good choice. Become familiar with the Dirty Dozen Plus™ list (a list of produce high in pesticides, like strawberries and peaches), and judge for yourself what works for you. If you can, focus on buying organic vegetables and fruit listed as the most contaminated and pick the type that's best for you, your circumstances, and any other personal considerations.

What is the *Dirty Dozen Plus™* list? Compiled by Environmental Working Group, this list will help you determine which fruits and vegetables have the most pesticide residues and are the most important to buy organic. The list can be found for free at http://www.ewg.org/foodnews/summary.php if you scroll to the bottom of the page. You can also get their *Shopper's Guide to Pesticides in Produce™* for a $10 donation.

CHAPTER 4

STOCKING A GLUTEN-FREE PANTRY ON A BUDGET

BASIC GLUTEN-FREE PANTRY STOCKING ITEMS

Having these basic items on hand in your kitchen will make cooking much easier! You can easily whip meals together as you become more comfortable.

Fats
- For drizzling and cooking: extra virgin olive oil
- For cooking and baking: organic extra virgin coconut oil
- Other oils for variety: avocado, grape seed, walnut, sesame

Sea Salt

Spices
Options are numerous. Don't stock your spice rack with every spice you can find. Keep your favorites on hand and maybe try one new spice a month. Here is a list of spices I use most often:

- Black pepper
- Onion powder
- Garlic powder
- Pumpkin pie spice

- Cinnamon
- Cumin powder
- Chili powder
- Paprika
- Crushed red pepper

Dried Herbs

Again, keep it simple. The most budget-friendly method is to grow and dry your own herbs. Here are a few of my go-to herbs:

- Rosemary
- Oregano
- Thyme
- Bay leaf
- Dill

Condiments

Condiments are tricky. Carefully read labels and verify with companies for gluten-free status of their products. Here are a few condiments to have on hand.

- Vinegar (balsamic, red wine, apple cider)
- Gluten-free tamari
- Coconut aminos
- Grey Poupon mustard
- Stevia (try Liquid Vanilla Crème stevia by SweetLeaf)
- Raw honey
- Pure vanilla extract

Vegetables

- Alliums: onion, garlic, leek, chives
- Starchy: sweet potato, winter squash (butternut, spaghetti, acorn)
- Roots: carrot, beet, parsnip, radish, daikon
- Sweet Bell pepper: green, red, yellow, orange
- Summer squash: zucchini, yellow squash
- Gluten-free frozen varieties

Dried Sea Vegetables

- Kombu (see Legumes section on how to use)
- Kelp flakes, dulse flakes (sprinkle on salads, add to soups)
- Nori sheets (for making rolls)

Gluten-Free Grains

- Rice: brown, wild, jasmine, basmati
- Quinoa
- Millet
- Oats

IMPORTANT

Oats are inherently gluten-free, but are frequently contaminated by wheat during growing and/or processing. Ask your physician if oats are acceptable for you.

Canned Items

- Beans: black beans, chickpeas, white beans (e.g. navy)
- Tomato: diced tomatoes, tomato paste
- Soup (read ingredients and look for "gluten-free" on label)
- Tuna, salmon (packed in water or oil only)
- Organic coconut milk: Try to find a brand that ideally contains only coconut and water as ingredients.

Dried Beans and Legumes

- Lentils (split or whole): red, green, yellow
- Beans: black turtle, aduki, mung
- Peas: split, whole

Fresh and Frozen Fish and Seafood

- Salmon (preferably wild-caught)
- Tilapia
- Cod

- Trout
- Shrimp
- Scallops

Raw, Pre-Shelled Nuts & Seeds

To preserve freshness and to avoid rancidity, store raw, pre-shelled nuts and seeds in airtight bags or containers in the freezer.

- Almond
- Pecan
- Walnut
- Pine nut
- Sunflower seed
- Pepita (pumpkin seed)

Coconut products

- Unsweetened shredded coconut
- Coconut flakes (roasted or raw)
- Coconut butter
- Organic extra virgin coconut oil
- Coconut aminos (in place of soy or tamari)
- Coconut cream
- Organic coconut milk

Fruit

Possibilities are endless. Stick with low glycemic fresh or frozen fruit. Avoid dried fruit because of their concentrated sugar content.

- Avocado
- Apple
- Citrus: lemon, lime, grapefruit
- Pear
- Berries: blueberry, strawberry, raspberry, etc.
- Plum

Bone Broth / Stock

When buying pre-made broth or stock, read the labels to be sure they are gluten-free and low-sodium or sodium-free. The healthiest and most cost-effective method is to make your own.

- Broth in Tetra Paks
- Bouillon cubes

Meat & Protein

Local grass-fed organic meat is your healthiest option. Buy meat when it is on sale. Always store uncooked meat in the freezer if you will not use within two days of purchase.

- Sausage
- Chicken pieces
- Pork tenderloin
- Beef cuts
- Eggs

Refer to Chapter 7 for more information on how to store and cook meat.

Storage Items

- Aluminum foil
- Parchment paper
- Wax paper
- Plastic wrap
- 2 or 3 different size heavy duty (freezer grade) zipper lock bags
- BPA-free plastic containers
- Glass jars (use tempered glass for freezing)

Refer to Chapter 5 for more information on how to use these storage options.

REMEMBER!

It is ultimately your responsibility to read labels and package ingredients of all pre-packaged and/or processed food products that you purchase (e.g. a bag of nuts, frozen peas, ground coffee, a jar of olives). Never assume it is safe simply because it should only be one ingredient. When in doubt, call the manufacturer to double check the product's gluten-free status.

This list is intended as a guide; however, you must double check products you buy and never assume that the product you bought two months ago is the same formulation as the one you'll buy tomorrow. Ingredients and manufacturing practices can and do change. Always read the label.

CHAPTER 5
FOOD STORAGE OPTIONS & TIPS

J UST AS IT IS CRUCIAL to know how to prepare and cook your food, it is also important to know how to properly store it. This is especially important when cooking in bulk (sticking extras in the freezer for another time) or for leftovers (sticking extras in the fridge for another time).

The only reliable way to remember when to use your leftovers by is to write it down. Cut a strip of masking tape (i.e. sticky tape or painter's tape), stick it on the bag or container, and write the date you've stored the item so you know when you placed it in the freezer and if it's been sitting for much too long.

> **GF SAVVY TIP**
> *Keep a list in your kitchen (ideally attached to the fridge) where you can keep track of what you have stored in your freezer for quick reference.*

Here are some of the types of containers you can store food in:

BPA-FREE PLASTIC CONTAINERS

These are a versatile must-have when cooking lots of leftovers. You can find these at all price points. More expensive brands are more durable (and some come with lifetime guarantees), but even cheaper brands are sturdy enough for everyday use. Containers with snap-on lids are best for solid food that will not be moved around, and twist-on lids are best for transporting food (e.g. in a lunch box) and storing liquids like soups, sauces, dressings, etc. Plastic containers tend to "absorb" whatever was last stored in them. It's worth taking a moment to sniff the inside of the container to make sure your fruit salad won't take on a taste of the spaghetti sauce you stored last, or your smoothie doesn't have a hint of the salad dressing you packed last time.

Caution*: Transfer food stored in plastic containers to a plate <u>before</u> heating in the microwave.*

Pantry: Dry ingredients and non-perishable liquids (e.g. honey and coconut nectar) can be put in labeled plastic containers in the pantry.

Fridge: Non-acidic ingredients and foods are best kept in labeled plastic containers in the fridge.

Freezer: Anything and everything can be put in labeled plastic containers in the freezer.

> ## GF SAVVY TIP
> *Food expands when it freezes, so always leave about one inch of head space in your container before placing in the freezer or the container may deform or crack.*

Marinating: Marinating usually involves ingredients like lemon juice or vinegar. These acidic ingredients tend to "eat away" at plastic, so I do not recommend using plastic containers for marinating more than 30 minutes. Zipper lock bags are best to use when marinating.

GLASS JARS

Tempered glass (freezer-safe) does not shatter in the freezer, however other types of glass can shatter. Make sure you know what type of glass container you are using before placing it in your freezer. For some people, glass is the only way to go. The great thing is that glass doesn't absorb the taste of what was last stored nor is it affected by acidic foods (lids and covers are a different story, so check them before reusing).

Pantry: Store all sorts of dry goods (e.g. nuts, seeds, dried fruit, dried spices, dried or powdered baking ingredients, uncooked grains, uncooked beans, and legumes) and non-perishable liquids (e.g. honey, sugar) in labeled and tightly covered glass jars.

Fridge: Store anything in labeled glass jars or bowls. Glass jars are especially useful for storing soups, broths, dressings, and sauces in the fridge.

Freezer: Anything and everything can be put into labeled tempered (freezer-safe) glass jars and stored in the freezer. Remember to leave one inch of head space between the contents and the lid to allow for the food to expand without cracking or shattering the jar.

Marinating: Glass bowls are especially useful for marinating. Place everything in the bowl, mix it up, cover, and marinate in the fridge for the allotted time.

ZIPPER LOCK BAGS

Zipper-style bags are great when you don't have enough plastic containers or glass jars, or when you want to save space in the pantry, fridge, or freezer. They are not as sturdy as plastic or glass, but when you buy a good quality brand, you can place just about anything in there and they will safely store your food until ready to use.

GF SAVVY TIP

Rinse out and air-dry non-punctured plastic bags when ingredients have run out. You can then refill them with new ingredients.

Pantry: Store all sorts of dry goods in labeled zipper lock bags like nuts, seeds, dried fruit, dried spices, dried or powdered baking ingredients, uncooked grains, and uncooked beans and legumes.

GF SAVVY TIP

If pests (e.g. mice and ants) are a problem, all dried good must be stored in tightly closed glass jars or BPA-free plastic containers.

Fridge: Store anything in zipper-style bags that you would normally place in a plastic or glass container. Beware when storing liquids in bags—do not overfill, and place upright in a bowl just to be safe. As noted in Chapter 12 on Salad and Other Greens, you can store leafy greens in the fridge for up to a week in these types of bags.

Freezer: These are especially useful when saving up bones for bone broth, meat pieces or ground meat (cooked or raw), cooked beans/legumes, cooked grains, veggies (cooked or raw), some herbs, and fruit. If you opt to freeze liquids in bags, be sure they are securely closed and do not leak.

GF SAVVY TIP

When freezing liquids, place them on a flat surface in the freezer, like a cookie sheet or in a square cake pan. When completely frozen, remove the sheet or pan and stick your bag back in the freezer until ready to use.

Marinating: Bags are useful for marinating. Stick everything in the bag, mix it up, and marinate in the fridge for the allotted time (stick upright in a bowl to avoid leaking).

CHAPTER 6

VEGETABLES

IF YOU HAVE BEEN FOLLOWING ME at GlutenFreeSchool. com, you know how much importance I put on eating whole food—especially vegetables. They should be the main attraction on your plate. Pack meals with as many vegetables as you can. Actually, vegetables should make up half (or more) of your plate.

Use vegetables to add color to your meals. Use vegetables to expand or bulk up main dishes. They are highly versatile. Add them to soups, stews, chili, casseroles, salads, and more. Throw them in your slow cooker, pressure cooker, frying pan, etc.

If you're not sure about adding and trying lots of new vegetables, keep things simple and make one huge serving of one type of vegetable to start. Each week, experiment by mixing in different vegetables to find your new favorites.

"But, I/my kids don't like vegetables!"

This comes up a lot, especially in households where processed foods have been a big part of the family diet. The only way to get around this is to eat vegetables anyway. Your tastes WILL change.

Here are some of my favorite ways to get more vegetables into your life:

- Do you or your family like at least one vegetable? Start with that.
- Slowly add other sweet-tasting vegetables, like carrots, sweet

potatoes, sugar snap peas, cherry tomatoes, buttercup or acorn squash, and red pepper.

- Experiment by preparing vegetables all different ways: steamed, fried, boiled, braised, roasted, sautéed, stir-fried, grilled, broiled and, of course, raw.
- Add spices to vegetable dishes to make them more interesting. Salt and pepper are basics, but don't be afraid to add variety by sprinkling a little basil, nutmeg (delicious on squash), garlic powder, or dill, to suggest a few.
- Serve cooked vegetables with olive oil or melted butter/ghee drizzled over top.
- "Hide" vegetables in food, such as smoothies, sauces, soups, and chili. Use an immersion blender to blend the vegetables together so no one notices!
- Instead of serving sauces or chili over rice or vermicelli, make cauliflower rice or spaghetti squash and see how pleasantly surprised everyone is!
- When making egg dishes, like omelets or frittatas, fry up onion, pepper, mushroom, and zucchini, add them to the egg and serve it all over a bed of baby spinach.
- Pack school and work lunches with baby cucumber, sliced peppers, baby carrots, broccoli or cauliflower florets, and lettuce wraps (food wrapped in lettuce leaves).

The more you "practice" adding vegetables to every meal, the easier it gets and the more you and your family will enjoy vegetables. Make it your goal to add more vegetables to your daily diet, and you will find countless ways to do so. You and your family will also discover new favorites, which you can come back to again and again.

FRESH VEGETABLES

As noted earlier, when shopping for fresh vegetables, go to produce stores first. Look for inexpensive vegetables, such as tubers and root vegetables like sweet potatoes, carrots, beets, onions, and garlic.

When buying fresh vegetables, purchase what is grown locally and in season.

By adding vegetables like summer squashes, carrots, and greens to soups, stews, chili, casseroles, and the slow cooker, you can freeze them, which makes your life easier.

COOKING FRESH VEGETABLES

Boil: For every two cups of vegetables, bring ¼ to ½ cup water with ½ teaspoon sea salt to a boil. Add vegetables, cover, and return to boil. As soon as the water returns to boiling, reduce heat and simmer gently until vegetables are fork tender. Drain well before serving.

Heat up: Microwave, on top of a double boiler, or steam until vegetables are fork tender.

Pan fry: Melt butter, ghee, or coconut oil (one tablespoon for every one cup of vegetables) in frying pan over medium heat. Add fresh vegetables, season, and fry over medium heat, stirring occasionally until just tender.

Bake/Roast: Most fresh vegetables can be baked with a roast or in a casserole in the oven. They can also be roasted on a lightly greased oven-safe baking dish, seasoned, covered, and baked at 325°F until tender, stirring at least once.

EASY METHOD FOR SAVING FRESH GARLIC

Mince an entire head of garlic and add it to a glass jar. Pour olive oil over top until the garlic is completely covered and sealed in. Cover with an airtight lid and store in the fridge up to four weeks. Scoop out whatever you need for a recipe requiring garlic. Having already minced garlic on hand like this cuts down on preparation time and saves money by using the entire garlic bulb with no waste.

FROZEN VEGETABLES

We all know that fresh is best; however, fresh is not always feasible. Maybe you live in a place where the fresh vegetables aren't up to snuff or prices are downright outrageous. This is where frozen vegetables can play a huge role. They are a great substitute, or even addition, when you need a meal to go the extra mile.

Check out your local grocery store for sales on frozen vegetables. If you have cold winter months, frozen vegetables allow you to add vegetables to your meals without buying expensive items grown halfway around the world. Frozen vegetables are a great way to bulk up your meals and get more nutrition from real food rather than focusing on refined grains and carbohydrates.

Frozen Vegetable Blends

Blends such as California Mix or Asian blends can be a great and easy way to add lots of color and flavor to your meals in a pinch, however you want to make sure that the blends are only vegetables. Do not buy blends pre-spiced or mixed with sauces as they may not be gluten-free.

As we all have different levels of gluten sensitivity, I always recommend reading labels to learn how the frozen vegetables you are selecting were handled and processed. If you ever have a question about gluten contamination, check the product's website and call the manufacturer to verify their gluten-free status.

Make sure the ingredient list ONLY includes the veggies and nothing else added.

FREEZING VEGETABLES

We talked about how to save money by freezing your own vegetables in Chapter 3. Buying vegetables in bulk when they are in season and when they come on special in your area is one of the best ways you can save money.

GF SAVVY TIP

Freezing is not recommended for artichokes, Belgian endive, eggplant, lettuce greens, radishes, sprouts, and sweet potatoes.

Simple Cut & Freeze Method

Most vegetables will last up to one month in the freezer using my *Simple Cut & Freeze Method*. If you want vegetables to last longer than one month in the freezer, follow my *Year-Long Frozen Vegetable Blanching Method* instructions in the next heading.

Here is a list of vegetables that will last for up to one month by simply cutting and freezing them:

- Onion
- Garlic
- Ginger
- Celery
- Pepper (sweet and spicy)
- Peas
- Asparagus
- Green beans
- Wax beans
- Okra

Instructions for *Simple Cut & Freeze Method*:

1. **Prepare**: Select vegetables listed above at their peak of freshness. Wash all vegetables thoroughly before beginning. Prepare for the fourth step by having lots of medium or large heavy duty zipper lock bags or freezer-safe containers. Unblanched (cut and frozen) raw vegetables store well frozen for about one month, so remember to write the expiration date on freezer bags or containers BEFORE packing them.
2. **Cut**: Chop, slice, or leave vegetables whole and spread them in a single layer on a parchment-lined pan or cookie sheet.
3. **Chill**: Stick in the freezer until vegetables are frozen solid, about one hour. Freeze as soon as possible after chilling.

4. **Pack & Freeze**: Take the pan out of the freezer. Use a knife to break pieces that may have clumped together. Use the parchment paper as a funnel to pour the chilled vegetables into labeled heavy duty zipper lock freezer bags or plastic containers. Remove excess air, then place in freezer. For best results, do not freeze more than three pounds at a time.

Repeat steps One through Four until all vegetables are chilled, packed, and stored in the freezer. When you want to add vegetables to cooked dishes or use them for frying, simply break up the vegetables in the bag and pour into your meal—no need to defrost!

GF SAVVY TIP

Do not use frozen vegetables where raw vegetables are needed, like in salads or dressings.

Year-Long Frozen Vegetable Blanching Method

Most vegetables will last up to a year in the freezer using my *Year-Long Frozen Vegetable Blanching Method*.

Why blanching? Blanching prevents enzymes from damaging color, flavor, and nutrients. The heat of boiling water also destroys harmful microorganisms that may be lingering on the surface of vegetables. Pack vegetables tightly to avoid air contact.

For an easier method, or if you only need vegetables to last one month or less in the freezer, follow the *Simple Cut & Freeze Method* instructions in the previous heading.

Refer to the *Gluten Free School Blanching & Cooking Guide* below for a list of vegetables and blanching times.

Take these steps when freezing vegetables for more than one month:

1. **Prepare**: Select vegetables that are at their peak of freshness. Wash all vegetables thoroughly before beginning. Prepare for the third step by thoroughly washing your sink (or a large bowl) and filling it with cold, clean water. Have ice cubes ready.

Prepare for the fourth step by having lots of large heavy duty zipper lock bags or freezer-safe containers. Vegetables store well frozen for about 12 months, so remember to write the expiration date on freezer bags or containers BEFORE packing them. (*Extra preparation step for asparagus, broccoli, Brussels sprouts, and cauliflower:* To remove insects that may be present, immerse prepared vegetables for 15 minutes in four cups water containing one tablespoon salt. Rinse thoroughly. Blanch as directed.)

2. **Blanch**: Not all vegetables need to be blanched as you will notice in the table below. Blanching vegetables before freezing preserves their quality by destroying enzymes, which can alter their color, texture, and flavor during freezing. In a large covered pot, bring water to a rolling boil. Use 16 cups for every pound of vegetables; use 32 cups of water for leafy vegetables. Place vegetables in a wire basket or hanging cheesecloth and lower gently into boiling water, making sure all vegetables are submerged. Stir. Cover and begin to count blanching time (in table below). Keep on high heat to quickly return water to a boil. Do not over- or under-blanch.

3. **Chill**: Once blanching is complete, remove vegetables from boiling water and immediately submerge vegetables into ice-cold water to halt the cooking process. Drain cooled vegetables to remove as much water as possible (a salad spinner is helpful for this). Freeze as soon as possible after chilling.

4. **Pack & Freeze**: Place chilled vegetables in labeled heavy duty zipper lock freezer bags or plastic containers. Remove excess air, then place in freezer. For best results, do not freeze more than three pounds at a time.

GLUTEN FREE SCHOOL BLANCHING & COOKING GUIDE	
Vegetable	**Blanching Time**
Asparagus, medium stalks cut in 2" (5 cm)	3 minutes
Beans (green or wax), cut in 1" (2.5 cm) pieces	3 minutes
Beet greens, tough stems removed	2 minutes (keeps for 6 months frozen)
Broccoli, medium stalks	3 minutes
Brussels Sprouts, medium size	4 minutes
Cabbage, cut in wedges	2 minutes
Carrots, cubed, sliced or in strips	3 minutes
Cauliflower, cut in 1" (2.5 cm) pieces	3 minutes
Celery, cut in 1" (2.5 cm) pieces	3 minutes
Peas (regular), shelled	2 minutes (keeps for 5 months frozen)
Peas (edible pods), strings removed	2 minutes (keeps for 5 months frozen)
Pepper (green or red), stem and seeds removed, cut in slices or rings	4 minutes
Rutabaga, Turnip, peeled, diced, boiled until tender	3 minutes
Squash (acorn, butternut, hubbard), seeded and peeled, cubed	2 minutes
Spinach	
Zucchini (yellow squash), cut in ½" slices	4 minutes

Beets: Remove tops leaving a 1-inch stem. Cook in boiling water until tender (25 to 30 minutes for small beets, 45 to 50 for medium beets). Cool, drain, peel, slice, or cube. Pack and freeze.

Garlic: Peel. Use *Simple Cut & Freeze Method*. Keeps for two months frozen.

Mushrooms: Trim ends of stems. Slice or quarter. Sauté 2 cups in 2 tablespoons butter, ghee, or coconut oil for 4 minutes. Cool, pack and freeze.

Onions: Remove outer skin, root, and stem ends. Chop. Use *Simple Cut & Freeze Method.* Keep frozen for 3 to 6 months.

Peppers (green or red), for use in salads and garnishes: Remove stem and seeds. Cut into slices or rings. Use *Simple Cut & Freeze Method.*

Spaghetti squash: Cut in half. Remove seeds. Place in baking pan with 1 inch of water and bake at 450F degrees for 45 minutes until tender. Cool. Pull with fork to make strands. Pack and freeze. Keep frozen for up to 9 months.

Tomatoes: Blanch for 30 seconds. Cool. Remove skin. Cut in half and remove seeds. Pack and freeze.

THAWING & COOKING FROZEN VEGETABLES

Thawing Frozen Vegetables

The nice thing about frozen vegetables is that most vegetables do not need to be thawed before cooking. Because frozen vegetables require less cooking time than fresh vegetables, they can be thrown into a meal a few minutes before serving.

Cooking Frozen Vegetables

You cannot use frozen vegetables to eat uncooked (for example, placing frozen red peppers in a lunch box for snack). You can, however, cook frozen vegetables in many different ways, such as boiling, microwaving, pan frying, or baking. To retain the flavor and health benefits of blanched vegetables, cook until just barely tender. Overcooking them is a sin!

Boil: For every two cups of frozen vegetables, bring ¼ to ½ cup water with ½ teaspoon sea salt to a boil. Add vegetables, cover, and return to boil. As soon as the water returns to boiling, reduce heat and simmer gently until vegetables are fork tender. Drain well before serving.

Reheat: Microwave, on top of a double boiler, or steam.

Pan fry: Melt butter, ghee, or coconut oil (one tablespoon for each one cup vegetables) in frying pan over medium heat. Add frozen vegetables, season, and fry over medium heat, stirring occasionally until just tender.

Bake/Roast: Most frozen vegetables can be baked with a roast or in a casserole in the oven. They can also be roasted on a lightly greased oven-safe baking dish, seasoned, covered, and baked at 325°F until tender, stirring at least once.

CANNED VEGETABLES

I'm not a fan of canned vegetables so I do not advise you to buy them. They are usually soggy and don't taste fresh which makes them undesirable to most people. The cans used by food companies are often lined with BPA and the contents often contain too much sodium and other unhealthy additives. For these reasons, it's my suggestion to buy frozen vegetables rather than the canned varieties.

QUESTIONABLE FOODS

Certain foods which are genetically modified deserve a bit more explanation and a cautionary word. Genetically modified foods (or GMO for short) or crops have been tinkered with by scientists to produce varying desirable effects such as increasing yield and making plants resistant to viruses or dying after being sprayed by toxic pesticides.

The general sentiment is that GMOs aren't good for us or the planet. An increasingly vocal movement opposed to GMO crops has been making successful strides to educate consumers to their potentially hazardous effects on both the body as well as the environment and convince food companies to stop using them in products. Legislation is also making GMO crops more visible both around the world and in certain states of the US.

I recommend that you do your best to stay away from as many GMO food crops as possible. With that said, the following two foods deserve a word of caution.

Corn

To be truthful, I am not the biggest fan of corn. There are several issues that come with cross-reactions to similar proteins found in gluten aside from the fact that corn is very starchy and highly glycemic. It is also difficult for many people with compromised digestive systems to break down corn. Also, non-organic varieties tend to be genetically modified (also known as a GMO) and produce very harsh chemicals within every cell of the corn plant, including that which we eat.

Edamame

If you can tolerate soy and do not suffer from any thyroid conditions, edamame can add a nice protein boost to many meals. This is one instance where I highly recommend buying organic as the non-organic variety tends to be genetically modified. However, there are some brands labeled organic that are highly suspect because the soybeans are grown in China where there are no organic standards. Whole Foods Market brands (as of the time I am writing this book) sell organic edamame from China, so the lesson here is to look for the country of origin to determine whether this is something you want to buy or not.

CHAPTER 7
MEAT, SEAFOOD & EGGS

A S FAR AS MEAT IS CONCERNED, **dark meat carries more flavor and is significantly less expensive than white meat**. Do not be afraid to buy dark meat on the bone, with the skin on. It's a misconception that perfectly clean, cut and filleted light meat is better. In actuality, it is healthier having meat on the bone with skin because you are consuming meat in its natural state. It's not to say that when you roast a chicken, you must eat the skin. But if you slow cook the chicken in a Crock Pot, or you make broth, leave it all on so that those good nutrients end up on your plate.

One way to get the biggest bang for your buck is to **use a whole chicken**. You can start off roasting it for a meal. When you're done, remove all the meat and save for leftovers. Then take the carcass and make stock from it cooking it over the stove or in a slow cooker. Though this may not sound very appealing to some people (stock is definitely a cultural thing), think of the money you will save by using homemade broth compared to paying $3 or $4 for store-bought stuff that has too many funky ingredients to name. I make all of my own broth. One chicken carcass makes, on average, the equivalent of eight to ten Tetra Pak containers (each contains about four cups), which I store in my freezer. That's at least $40 saved right there and it lasts in the freezer for about three months.

If you roast chicken pieces rather than a whole chicken, store the bones in a freezer bag and save them in your freezer. When you have enough, take them out and use them to make stock.

In supermarkets, **look for inexpensive parts like ox tail, chicken necks, or marrow bones**. They add wonderful flavor to soups and stocks. Don't shy away from cooking with these items just because they seem weird or unappetizing. In reality, they make really good food and the nutrients they provide are incredibly healthy.

> **GF SAVVY TIP**
> *Save money and eat healthier, more nutrient-dense food by making your own stocks and soups from bones and meat.*

Look for meat that's close to being expired. Grocery stores typically discount meat near its expiration date because it is less desirable. The bonus for you is that you can sometimes find meat at up to 50 percent off. If you do not need to use the meat right away, stick it in the freezer. Then pull out your desired cut of meat when you need it. Allow it the time to defrost and then cook it.

Tougher cuts of meat are also usually less expensive. These cuts of meat tenderize when they are slow cooked in a Crock Pot. Slow cook overnight or all day while you're at work. When you get home, you have this large, lovely vat of whatever it is you cooked up—a soup, a stew, a chili, a pot roast—and serve it for supper. Compliment it with rice, beans, and vegetables. By doing so, you allow the food to go a long way, and you've made a flavorful meal without too much effort.

MEAT & SEAFOOD INTERNAL COOKING TEMPERATURE GUIDE

Help protect you and your family from foodborne illness by using a digital food thermometer to ensure that raw meat, seafood, and poultry are cooked to a safe internal temperature.

Here are a few tips to follow:

- After cooking, remove your food from heat and let it sit for at least 3 minutes. Then insert a digital food thermometer through the thickest part of the meat, all the way to the middle.

- Avoid a false reading by ensuring the thermometer does not touch any bones (they heat up quicker than the meat).
- Temperatures may differ in different pieces, so check each piece separately.
- For hamburgers, insert the digital food thermometer through the side of the patty, all the way to the middle.

Use this handy chart when checking to see if your meat has reached the necessary, safe internal cooking temperature.

GLUTEN FREE SCHOOL MEAT & SEAFOOD INTERNAL TEMPERATURE GUIDE	
Beef, veal, lamb	**Internal Temperature**
Medium-rare	145°F / 63°C
Medium	160°F / 71°C
Well done	170°F / 77°C
Pork	**Internal Temperature**
Pieces and whole cuts	160°F / 71°C
Ground meat; Meat mixes	**Internal Temperature**
Ground beef, veal, lamb, pork	160°F / 71°C
Ground poultry	165°F / 74°C
Poultry	Internal Temperature
Pieces	165°F / 74°C
Whole	185°F / 85°C
Seafood	**Internal Temperature**
Fish	158°F / 70°C
Shellfish	165°F / 74°C

Refer to this site for a complete list of foods:
http://www.foodsafety.gov/keep/charts/mintemp.html

MEAT STORAGE GUIDE

If the package doesn't have a 'best before' date, use this handy chart to know how long fresh food and leftovers will last.

GLUTEN FREE SCHOOL MEAT STORAGE GUIDE			
Food		Refrigerator 40°F / 4°C	Freezer 0°F / -18°C
Fresh, uncooked beef, veal, lamb, pork	Steaks	3-4 days	6-12 months
	Shops	3-4 days	4-6 months
	Roasts	3-5 days	4-12 months
Fresh, uncooked ground beef or stew cubes		1-2 days	2-4 months
Fresh, uncooked ground turkey, veal, lamb, pork		1-2 days	3-4 months
Fresh, uncooked chicken and turkey	Whole	1-2 days	1 year
	Pieces	1-2 days	6-9 months
Uncooked bacon (use by 'best before' date)		7 days	1 month
Eggs	Fresh, Raw	Use by 'Best Before' date	4 months (blended eggs)
	Hard cooked	1 week	Not recommended
Fish	Cooked	1-2 days	4-6 months
	Fatty fish (salmon, tuna, striped bass, etc.)	2-3 days	2-3 months
	Fresh lean fish (cod, flounder, haddock, halibut, perch)	2-3 days	3-6 months
	Opened canned fish	1 day	Not recommended
Leftover cooked meat	Meat and casseroles	3-4 days	2-3 months
	Broth	3-4 days	2-3 months
	Poultry casseroles	3-4 days	4-6 months
	Plain poultry pieces	3-4 days	4 months
Soups and stews (with meat or vegetables)		3-4 days	2-3 months

CHAPTER 8

LEGUMES & BEANS

IF YOU FEEL MEAT IS EXPENSIVE (and it is), look no farther than the lowly and often under-appreciated legume—lentils, peas, and beans. A gluten-free vegetarian or vegan diet will require beans for added protein and variety.

The most common legumes are lentils, peas, mung beans, soybeans, and chickpeas. Dry legumes are on average twice as rich in protein as grains, and are typically a good source of iron and B-vitamins. They are rich in fiber and good sources of complex carbohydrates. Lentils can be helpful for blood sugar control.

Legumes make a nice addition to a variety of dishes and are budget-friendly, especially if you're willing to cook them yourself (as opposed to buying the canned variety). From chickpeas to lentils and black turtle beans to kidney beans, legumes come in a wide range of flavors, sizes, and colors. They are a sensational addition to cooking, from salads to sauces, soups to casseroles—the possibilities are endless!

If you know that you'll be home for a couple hours during the weekend, for example, soak some beans overnight. The following day, rinse them well and then cook them up. Cooking them couldn't be easier. Yes, soaking and cooking can take time, but you are not doing much work—they just sit on your stovetop.

CANNED VS. DRIED

Answer this question: *Do you prefer saving money in exchange for spending more time in the kitchen or would you rather spend more money in exchange for convenience?*

If you prefer saving money on food, you know it means you need to spend a bit more time and effort in the kitchen.

Cooking dried legumes yourself saves you money.

The math is pretty simple: One bag of dried legumes at the grocery store is generally a dollar. The amount of beans in the bag doubles, sometimes triples in size, when cooked.

Compare that to one can of beans, which can range anywhere from maybe a dollar all the way up to three dollars a can, depending on whether you're buying organic or not.

Another consideration is that canned beans can be very high in sodium and have other unhealthy additives along with BPA (a hormone-disrupter leached from all pre-coated cans). If the ingredient list on the canned beans you are looking at has anything other than beans and water, it may not be the healthiest choice.

If you decide to use canned legumes, be sure to strain, rinse well, and drain for two minutes to reduce the sodium content as well as some of the gas-inducing carbohydrates and sugars.

ARE ALL LEGUMES GLUTEN-FREE?

Legumes are subject to significant gluten cross-contamination, which is a problem for people with celiac disease or non-celiac gluten sensitivity.

Some people will tell you to simply wash off traces of gluten, however it's not that easy—some gluten seems to remain, despite your best scrubbing efforts (even using soap).

Not all legume crops are highly cross-contaminated. However, it is a big enough problem that some companies call out the risk on the labels of their dried beans with the statement "May Contain Wheat". Have you ever found barley kernels in bags of dried lentils or other beans? I have.

That's why I highly recommend that anyone with celiac or gluten sensitivity—especially those sensitive to trace gluten—purchase only beans that have been certified gluten-free.

Certified Gluten-Free Beans

There are currently only two companies that I know of who sell certified gluten-free dried beans:

Shiloh Farms: This producer of organic and natural food products has a dedicated gluten-free production line for its certified products, including dried legumes. Shiloh Farms offers more than a dozen different bean varieties.
(http://www.shilohfarms.com/certified-gluten-free)

Nuts.com: Despite the name, Nuts.com offers more than just nuts. Gluten-free dried bean options are cranberry beans, fava beans, garbanzo beans, and cannellini beans.
(http://www.nuts.com/gluten-free/#certified)

There aren't many canned beans that are certified gluten-free, so I recommend sticking with dry bean varieties.

Bush's Best: This company's canned beans are gluten-free, according to their website. (http://www.bushbeans.com/en_US/faq.jsp)

COOKING DRIED LEGUMES

Cooking dried legumes is easy. These are the steps:

Pick through.

Remove any pebbles or discolored, broken, cracked, shriveled beans as they won't cook properly. Pick out a rogue bean or grain that may have slipped into the bag (read more about this above in *Are All Legumes Gluten-Free?*). The best way is to spread them on a tray for sorting.

Soak.

Dried beans and legumes, with the exception of split peas and lentils, require soaking in room-temperature water, a step that rehydrates them for more even cooking. Soaking legumes cuts cooking times by as much as 70 percent—think of the energy savings!

Soaking also helps break down oligosaccharides (indigestible sugars that cause gas in beans), as well as removing phytic acid which can leach certain micronutrients from your body.

Standard soak method:
In a stock pot, cover your desired amount of dried legumes so that there is three inches of water above the top of the legumes.

Cover and let sit. Refer to *Gluten Free School Dried Legume Cooking Guide* for soaking times.

Quick soak method:
In a stock pot, bring four cups of water to a boil.

Add 1 cup dried beans and return to a boil. Boil two to three minutes.

Cover and set aside at room temperature for 60 to 90 minutes.

Drain & Rinse.

Do NOT use the soaking water to cook the beans. Not only does it contain all the gas-causing, indigestible complex sugars of oligosaccharides that have leached out of the beans, but also all the junk that came off the beans.

Drain the soaking water and give them a final rinse before cooking.

Cook.

Cooking legumes is pretty straightforward. Add water and soaked beans to a pot, bring it to a boil, turn down heat, cover, and simmer.

To further reduce the gas-producing properties of beans, add a one-inch strip of dried kombu (a type of seaweed) to the pot of beans and water prior to boiling. Remove the kombu once cooking is finished. Adding a slice or two of ginger or some fennel or cumin seeds can also help to increase the digestibility of the beans. I also suggest skimming the surface and discarding the foam during boiling to further remove gas produced by the beans.

Cooking instructions:
Fill a saucepan with fresh cold water and soaked legumes (refer to *Gluten Free School Dried Legume Cooking Guide* for amount of water). Cover.

Bring to boil in a saucepan. Reduce to a very light simmer to prevent skins from bursting. Tilt the lid slightly to allow steam to escape and leave to cook for the designated time (refer to *Gluten Free School Dried Legume Cooking Guide* for cooking times).

Periodically check the beans and add more water if the water level goes below the beans. Do not allow the water to evaporate.

Beans are done when they are tender and can be easily mashed between two fingers or with a fork.

Drain
Most of the water will be absorbed during the cooking phase, but drain them, especially if you will be adding the cooked legumes to salads or using them as a garnish. All water needs to be drained from legumes before freezing them.

Serve
Add cooked legumes to soups, sauces, rice, salads, casseroles, chili, or mash them into dip.

Store
Store cooked legumes covered in the fridge for four to five days. Cooked legumes freeze well (except lentils) and can keep in the freezer for up to six months.

GLUTEN FREE SCHOOL DRIED LEGUME COOKING GUIDE

Legume	Soaking Time (cover with 3" water)	Cooking liquid per cup of legume	Cooking Time
Adzuki (aduki, azuki) beans	1 to 2 hours	4 cups	45 to 60 minutes
Anasazi beans	4 to 8 hours	3 cups	60 minutes
Black (Turtle, Mexican, Spanish) beans	Overnight	4 cups	60 to 90 minutes
Black-eyed peas	Quick Soak Method	3 cups	60 minutes
Cannellini (white kidney) beans	Overnight	4 cups	45 to 90 minutes
Chickpeas (garbanzo beans)	Overnight	4 cups	90 to 120 minutes
Dried peas, split	None	4 cups	30 to 60 minutes
Dried peas, whole	Overnight	6 cups	60 to 90 minutes
Fava (broad) beans	Overnight	3 cups	60 to 120 minutes
Kidney beans	Overnight	3 cups	Boil 10 minutes, simmer 60 to 90 minutes
Lentils, Green (Le Puy) or Brown	None	2 cups	30 to 45 minutes
Lentils, Red (masoor dal) or Yellow	None	2 cups	15 to 30 minutes
Lima beans	Overnight	4 cups	60 minutes
Lima beans, Baby	6 to 8 hrs	4 cups	45 min – 60 min
Navy (Yankee) beans, Peas, Haricot	Overnight	3 cups	60 to 90 minutes
Pinto beans	Overnight	3 cups	60 to 90 minutes
Tepary beans	Overnight	3 cups	90 minutes

FREEZING COOKED LEGUMES

Because one bag of dried legumes yields such a large quantity when cooked, some might wonder what to do with leftovers. The answer: Freeze them!

Yes, you can freeze beans. When cooking beans for a specific recipe, make more than you need and freeze the rest.

Freezing cooked legumes is simple:

1. If freshly cooked, immerse them in cold water until cool.
2. Rinse and drain them well (drain at least two minutes).
3. Put them in a labeled freezer bag (they last for up to six months, so write the expiration date before adding legumes to the bag). Fill bags with no more than two cups of cooked legumes.
4. Squeeze most of the air out of the bag.
5. Store them in the freezer for up to six months.

If you want to be absolutely certain they will not clump together into a solid block, spread cooked legumes in a single layer on a parchment-lined pan or cookie sheet. Stick in the freezer until legumes are frozen, about one hour. Take the pan out of the freezer and use the parchment paper as a funnel to pour the legumes in labeled heavy duty zipper lock freezer bags, plastic containers, or tempered glass jars. Place in freezer for up to six months.

When you're ready to use them, take the bag, container, or jar out of the freezer, break up frozen beans with your hands, and pour them into whatever you're cooking. They are already cooked so it should take about three minutes to defrost them in whatever heated dish you've added them to.

If you add frozen legumes to salads, let them defrost on the counter for a few hours or microwave them in 15 second intervals until they are room temperature.

SPROUTING LEGUMES

Sprouts are one of the most economical foods and some have called them the food of the future. Sprouting your own legumes is so simple, and yields such savings and benefits, I cannot recommend it enough.

In colder climates, grow sprouts during the winter months to get hard-to-find nutrition without spending a lot of money on produce.

You can eat a variety of different beans and sprouts that you might not be able to buy in stores if you sprout them yourself.

Sprouting instructions:
1. Start by purchasing organic dry beans. Choose garbanzo beans (chickpeas), lentils, peas, and mung beans.
2. Soak beans overnight in a bowl with clean, fresh water.
3. The next morning, drain water and rinse with clean, fresh water until water runs clear.
4. Add the beans in a colander to sprout, rinsing them every 8 to 12 hours. Place a plate under the colander and cover the colander with a towel to keep debris out.
5. Every morning and night rinse with fresh water to keep the sprouts wet and clean. Ensure the sprouts never dry out.
6. The length of time for sprouting will depend on the temperature in your home. In cooler weather, it can take up to 24 hours for a tiny sprout to peek through, but in warmer climates, it can start within 12 hours. If a seed will not sprout, this is an indication that it is "dead" and the enzymes in it have been destroyed. Remove it from the sprouting batch and throw away (or compost).
7. Repeat the rinsing process until "tails" reach desired length.
8. When ready to serve, rinse out with fresh water and serve immediately. Store in glass jars in the fridge. They can be served cold or cooked.

Sprouts make a great addition to any meal and they add a crunchy texture to salads.

As you get more proficient at sprouting, you may want to make a small investment in sprouting bags or jars.

ADDING COOKED AND SPROUTED LEGUMES TO MEALS

Here are some ideas on how to add legumes to your gluten-free diet:

- Add one cup of cooked or puréed legumes to your tomato sauce or chili and reduce the amount of ground meat used.
- Toss one cup of cooked or sprouted legumes with any salad for a different twist.
- Mix cooked or sprouted legumes with rice and herbs and serve as a side dish or main meal.
- Mix ½ cup of cooked legumes into one cup of gluten-free salsa. Add chopped cilantro and a squeeze of lime juice for an easy party dip. Serve with raw vegetables.
- Serve hummus (chickpea is the main ingredient) with carrots, celery, or other vegetables.
- Sauté onion and garlic with salt and spices, then mix with cooked legumes.
- Make a salad with cooked or sprouted legumes. Add celery, red onion, tomato, red wine vinegar, olive oil, black olives, and your favorite herbs. Options and variations are virtually endless.

You can also purchase certain beans (edamame, black eye peas, etc.) already frozen from certain companies. This is a great alternative to canned beans. Just beware of edamame coming from China as they may be genetically modified and growing using pesticides and dangerous chemicals.

CHAPTER 9
GRAINS

IF YOU EAT GRAINS, gluten-free grains are a great money-saving food item that add bulk to your meals. Buy them in bulk and store them in airtight glass jars or BPA-free plastic containers, out of the sunlight.

WHOLE GRAINS VS. REFINED GRAINS

I often get asked if there's really a difference between whole and refined grains. Yes, there certainly is! As people try to improve the quality of their diet, whole grains have become more popular and are now used in marketing labels on food products.

The biggest reason why whole grains are better than those which are refined is the nutritional impact. Whole grains have more fiber and breakdown less quickly during digestion which slows the impact of their carbohydrates on your blood sugar. Because there is more fiber, whole grains tend to take longer to cook, but the benefit of having a more stable blood sugar level after a meal is worth the extra wait.

As for the difference in taste and texture, whole grains are generally chewier than refined grains and have a nuttier, fuller flavor. If you are new to whole grains, you may find this unfamiliar at first. But after a month or two, refined grains may start to taste very plain and uninteresting by contrast. Stick with it until your palate adjusts, and reap the health benefits.

BULK COOKING

A shortcut I always recommend is to cook whole grains in big batches and save leftovers in labeled freezer bags or containers in the fridge or freezer.

Cooked grains keep three to four days in your fridge or four to six months in the freezer.

When you want some, pull the grains out of the fridge or freezer, take out what you need (it breaks up easily, even when frozen), and stick the rest back.

They take only a few minutes to warm up with a little added water or broth, in a soup or sauce, in a bag with hot water, or in the microwave.

Use leftover cooked grains for:

- Side dishes: Warm and serve.
- Salads: Toss cooked grains in with chopped veggies, dressing, and anything else you want.
- Soups, casseroles, or chili: Toss in a few handfuls near the end of cooking time.
- Sauces: Warm and serve with sauce.

APPROVED GLUTEN-FREE GRAINS

Rice is the most budget-friendly, gluten-free grain option. Supermarket sales and buying in bulk allow you to supplement and add variety with more expensive gluten-free grains such as quinoa, millet, and buckwheat.

Just a word of caution before you dive into the bulk bin aisle...

The **bulk bins in any grocery store are off limits** to those of us with food sensitivities and allergies unless you shop in a 100 percent gluten-free store. There are simply too many variables at play that could get you glutened even though something like nuts would naturally be gluten-free. Unbeknownst to you, the store may have put your naturally gluten-free items in a bin that has formerly stored wheat. Or the wheat flour in a container up higher could slowly settle downwards through the containers and end up in the bin of food you buy. And don't forget the customers who use the wrong spoons and tongs, which results in contamination.

When I refer to buying in bulk, I am referring to larger quantities of grains pre-packed by companies who clearly test and mark their products for gluten. Sometimes you can buy larger quantities at a reduced cost per pound by doing so. Amazon.com is a great online resource that allows you to purchase from some of your favorite companies and have everything delivered to you.

Here is the list of approved gluten-free grains:

- Amaranth
- Buckwheat
- Millet
- Oats
- Quinoa
- Rice
- Sorghum
- Teff
- Wild Rice

Rice & Quinoa
Cooked rice lasts about 5 days in the fridge and 4 to 6 months in the freezer.

There are all sorts of varieties of rice to choose from. In North America, the most common varieties found in stores are brown, basmati, jasmine, and Arborio. Choose whatever is readily available and affordable in your area.

Wild rice is not technically rice, but it is still very nutritious and cooks the same as rice.

Quinoa is a pseudo-grain/seed which originates from South America. It is typically cream-colored although there are also dark brown and red varieties. Always rinse quinoa well to remove the naturally occurring saponin residue from the outside which will make the grain taste bitter (and keeps the birds from eating it before the plant can spread its seeds).

Both rice and quinoa can be frozen in freezer bags. I always make extra to have on hand in a pinch since both defrost quickly and easily. Some stores even carry bags of frozen rice and quinoa now to make your life easier!

Oats

Though oats are technically gluten-free, they must be marked gluten-free because they are often grown, harvested, and processed near or on the same equipment as wheat. I've known people who have tested Quaker® Oats for gluten and they definitely are above the level of gluten that's considered safe for those with Celiac Disease (which the level of allowable gluten in gluten-free products is mandated by the U.S. FDA to be below 20 parts per million).

Not everyone who must be gluten-free can tolerate oats. The Celiac-Sprue Association does not consider oats to be part of a gluten-free diet, so anything marked with their seal is required to be both gluten- and oat-free.

You can find different degrees of processed oats that allow some to cook faster, but are less healthy for you. Quick-cooking oats that you can microwave in less than two minutes are the most processed. Rolled Oats are less processed, need a bit more cooking time, and would be used to make granola. Steel cut oats (or groats) are the least processed, but require more cooking time. They have more fiber and nutrients as a result.

COOKING GLUTEN-FREE GRAINS

Don't be intimidated by grains. Cooking most grains is very similar to cooking rice. You put the dry grain in a pan with water or broth, bring it to a boil, then simmer until the liquid is absorbed (can also be drained).

Grains can vary in cooking time depending on the age of the grain, the variety, and the pans you're using to cook. Consider the table below as a general guide.

When you decide they're tender and tasty, they're done! If the grain is not as tender as you like when the cook time has elapsed, simply add more water and continue cooking. If everything seems fine before the liquid is absorbed, drain the remaining liquid.

Read cooking instructions on the package. If you transfer your grains from their original package to glass or another container, be sure to place the cooking instructions from the package in your new container.

Shortcut Method of Cooking Grains
To cook grains more quickly, let them soak in the allotted amount of water for a few hours before cooking. Just before dinner, add extra water if necessary, then cook. You'll find that cooking time is much shorter with a little pre-soaking.

Guide to Cooking Grains

Grain (1 cup dry)	Water or Broth	Bring to a boil, then simmer for...	Yields this much cooked grains
Amaranth	2 cups	20-25 minutes	3½ cups
Buckwheat groats, toasted or untoasted	2 cups	20 minutes	4 cups
Millet, hulled	2½ cups	25-35 minutes	4 cups
Oats, steel cut	4 cups	20 minutes	4 cups
Quinoa (well rinsed), white, black or red	2 cups	12-15 minutes	3 cups (or more)
Rice, brown	2½ cups	25-45 minutes (varies by variety)	3-4 cups
Rice, wild	3 cups	45-55 minutes	3½ cups
Teff	3 cups	5-20 minutes	3½ cups

Because grains contain a lot of carbohydrates, watch your portion size and don't make grains the main part of the meal. Vegetables should be the main attraction.

Avoiding Grains?

Some people on a gluten-free diet opt to avoid grains entirely because they find that not only does gluten bother them, but so do other proteins and components found in the grains. By avoiding grains, a person would follow a Grain-Free diet.

Taking this a step further is the Paleo diet which abstains from both grains and legumes. These items are avoided (along with processed foods) because of their glycemic impact on the body as well as what are termed "anti-nutrients" such as phytic acid which may cause depletion of certain micronutrients as well as contribute to digestive issues such as Leaky Gut Syndrome.

If you still do not feel better after cleaning up your Gluten-Free Diet with the tips and tricks suggested in this book, you may want to consider trying out one of these diet options. They can be very helpful for those struggling with ongoing inflammation and chronic autoimmune issues.

CHAPTER 10:

SPICES & HERBS

PEOPLE TEND TO GET NERVOUS cooking gluten-free because of so many different flavor and texture variables. On top of this is the added pressure of now having to season your own food. If you have not taken lessons in cooking and avoid your kitchen like the plague, seasoning food is probably not your forté. Because you may not do much of it, the food you make doesn't taste so good. Salt and pepper are not the only spices available to you! By having an array of spices and herbs to choose from, your food will taste better and allow for more creativity as you develop a level of comfort in spicing dishes.

Consider buying your spices in their whole form. As soon as spices are ground, they start losing their flavor. For example, black peppercorns will last longer than a jar of pre-ground black pepper. If you buy whole spices, use a high-speed food processor or a spice (or coffee) grinder to grind up what you want in smaller batches.

Let's not forget herbs! They are an excellent addition to any meal and have added health benefits as well. Though it's tempting to buy dried herbs, the more tender herbs like parsley, cilantro and basil aren't worth purchasing dried. They do not have much flavor. They are best purchased fresh and used fresh (or frozen, as I will explain in a moment). Other herbs like sage, thyme, rosemary and oregano keep their flavor and are great to have on hand dried (especially in the winter).

I love to grow my own herbs. Though gardening might not be everybody's favorite thing to do (and perhaps you don't have the space), it is a great way to have fresh cheap herbs on hand whenever you need them. Herbs actually grow great in window pots since they don't need a lot of space to flourish. Stores such as The Home Depot®, Lowe's® or some sort of local gardening center carry plants that are already started. Make sure it gets the appropriate amount of sunlight and water it every few days, making sure that it doesn't dry out completely.

Every summer, I grow lots of basil plants. From a few dollars spent on a plant provides me fresh basil for the entire summer. I don't ever need to buy it which is incredibly cost effective and a real time-saver since the herbs are waiting for me a few steps away. You'll never end up wasting money so long as you give them a few moments of care each day. Otherwise you'll be left to purchase fresh herbs at the grocery store. One of my biggest grievances in doing so is that you always end up throwing so much of the plant away before you may be able to use it all which ultimately wastes money. When I buy a bunch of parsley, I probably never use more than half before what remains becomes unusable.

One plant that I can't recommend more to be the easiest herb to grow is rosemary. It loves the full sun, doesn't need much water at all and can survive through the winter. It's a perennial plant that's incredibly low maintenance. I have a lovely large bush I started from a $3 plant over five years ago outside of my home that can thrive in both 100° F summers and 30° F winters. I have never needed to purchase any more fresh or dried rosemary ever since planting it.

If you've got to get fresh herbs at the grocery store, don't let them go to waste! Pick out the part of the herb bunch that's still good, rinse it off and mince it up. You will need a sharp knife to chop everything. Then scoop the minced herbs into ice cube trays and fill the cubes up with water, just as if you were making ice. You can also use olive oil instead of water. Put the ice cube tray into the freezer until frozen. Once it's ready, pop out all the ice cubes and put them in a freezer bag. Anytime you need to add some fresh parsley or basil to a stew, soup, or to your meal, just throw the ice cube right in, and it will melt naturally. There you go! It's that easy to get fresh flavors into your meals.

This will keep you from throwing away perfectly good fresh herbs and the money spent on a small bunch of parsley or basil still keeps on giving instead of ending up in the trash.

CHAPTER II

FRUIT

D ID YOU KNOW that you can freeze fruit? Okay, well not all fruit, but a large majority of the most common fruit you purchase doesn't have to end up in the trash if you forget to eat it or it goes bad quicker than you anticipated. Also, you can save seasonal favorites for use later in the year.

Learning how to freeze fruit came about because I got tired of throwing away pints of strawberries that seemed to explode into fuzzy mold balls over night. If you're on a limited budget, healthier fruit like berries can be expensive to buy and feel even more expensive as it lands in the trash. After tossing too much fruit, I decided to become proactive and save it before it was completely unappetizing.

I have successfully frozen berries, pears, watermelon, bananas, peaches, and pretty much every other fruit. Though I've not frozen citrus fruit, it is possible to freeze lemon slices for adding to drinks and sparkling water. Truthfully, freezing fruit is incredibly simple, easy and will save you lots of money in the long run.

The general key to freezing fruit is to lay it out flat on a baking sheet or cutting board that's lined with wax or parchment paper. Pop everything into the freezer until the fruit is frozen. Then place it in a freezer bag and keep in the freezer for whenever you need it.

To get you started, here's how I handle some of my favorite fruit:

Cherries – Rinse, pit and freeze in a freezer bag.

Whole berries (blueberries, raspberries, blackberries, etc.) – Rinse, loosely dry with paper towels and freeze in a freezer bag.

Strawberries – Remove stem and leaves & rinse. Either keep whole or slice in to pieces and freeze in a freezer bag.

Larger fruit (peaches, pears, plums, nectarines) – Rinse and slice in halves or smaller slices/chunks. Spread on baking sheet lined with parchment or waxed paper and freeze. Then keep pieces frozen in freezer bags.

Bananas – Peel bananas and freeze in a freezer bag.

Melons (watermelon, cantaloupe, honeydew) – Remove the rind, cut into desired chunks, spread on baking sheet lined with parchment or waxed paper and freeze. Then keep pieces frozen in freezer bags.

PRACTICAL USES FOR FROZEN FRUIT

As I've already shared, throwing away fruit that's gone bad is one of my least favorite things to do. However, fruit which is slightly overly ripe can make very good frozen fruit because it's so naturally sweet. It might not be what you'd reach for to eat (like a dark brown-skinned banana), but it doesn't mean that it's necessarily bad.

Fruit that's overly ripe, but not yet moldy is usually ideal for freezing. By doing so, you greatly expand the window for when you must use the fruit. My general rule of thumb for using my own frozen fruit is within about two months or so long as it's not freezer burned. This allows summer favorites to last longer to be used through the autumn.

If you're not used to using frozen fruit, don't be afraid to get creative! It can easily be used for a variety of recipes. Here are a few ideas to try:

Make smoothies using frozen fruit. It also eliminates the need to add ice cubes if required in a recipe (since the fruit will make it cold enough).

Blend frozen fruit with water and summer herbs like mint to create refreshing fruity drinks in the warmer months.

Make your own healthy ice cream. If you own a Vitamix® or a Yonanas® Ice Cream Maker, you can use bananas, berries and peaches to make your own natural soft-serve ice cream which is much healthier and economical.

Microwave berries until defrosted and add to plain yogurt and granola to jazz up parfaits.

Sauté fruit and spices like cinnamon, nutmeg or pumpkin pie spice to create a quick, warming dessert topped with nuts.

MONEY-SAVING FRUIT TIPS

When fruit begins to get too ripe, some grocery and discount produce stores will mark fruit down in an effort to sell it before the fruit goes bad. That is a great opportunity to buy your favorite fruit at a discount and freeze it for later. A produce store near me sells bananas which are getting brown for $.10 per pound. I will pick up a couple of pounds to freeze.

Remember when you go on vacation, don't throw leftover fruit away. Freeze it and enjoy it when you get back!

CHAPTER 12
SALAD & OTHER GREENS

D ON'T YOU HATE IT when you buy a bag of salad greens
and then find them rotten a few days later in your fridge?
You're not alone. I, too, have been lured by the "Buy two
for the price of one" signs and then somehow forget about them
or am unable to even get through the first bag of greens before everything that's left in both has become a slimy mess. Salad greens
going bad are one of the greatest frustrations ever!

The reason the leaves don't hold their freshness is that greens pack-
aged in bags were picked from their root base quite a while ago.
This means that they are starting to wither away due to dehydra-
tion when you buy them. Companies fill the bags with different
gasses to try to maintain the leaves for a certain period of time.
Usually, those bags of greens are one of the biggest rip-off items
at the grocery store. They seem like a good deal, but they're really
not, especially if you are not going to use it all right away.

Even though it may seem like buying an entire head of lettuce is a
bit of a hassle and maybe even a tad more expensive, think again.
The head of lettuce (or any greens that still have roots attached)
will stay fresh longer and may have even more lettuce on it than
what's in a pre-washed bag.

HOW TO SAVE GREENS FOR SEVEN DAYS OR MORE!

When you get home, chop everything up and then wash it. I suggest getting a salad spinner so that you can easily wash the greens in the basket. Spin the greens well to remove most of the water and then put the chopped up greens into a zipper lock bag. You can really pack a lot in. "Vacuum seal" the bag by closing the zipper about ¾ of the way. Then press the bag against yourself so that you can slowly push out the air. Then slide the zipper all the way across quickly to keep the air out. Store your greens in the fridge for about seven days. As you remove greens for salads, make sure to "vacuum seal" the bag again before putting it back in the refrigerator.

Should you feel that the bag is becoming too moist (remember these leaves are still alive and breathing), add a paper towel to soak up some of the extra moisture and protect the contents of your bag from going bad.

Use this for spinach, arugula, all lettuces, endive, dandelion, escarole, kale, mustard greens, collard greens, beet greens, chard and more.

CHAPTER 13
HOME GARDEN

A GARDEN IS A GREAT WAY to reduce the amount of money you spend on food. If you have the space, consider adding plants that are attractive and edible over those which merely look pretty. I've already mentioned in Chapter 9 that herbs can be easily grown in pots, make meals interesting and can save you plenty of money each week. But there are some other great ideas to try as well which might also work.

Be aware that different plants have different lifespans. Annual plants only last for one year/growing season while perennial plants can live for more than two. Having a mix of the two can make your life easier. Always read the directions included with the plant if you're not familiar with what it will need to thrive and if you need more help, search the internet. I've learned a lot by simply typing into Google– "How do you grow _____ ".

Here are a few examples of plants that are low maintenance and cost effective:

Rosemary – A perennial plant that grows in full sun and doesn't require much care or water.

Sage – Depending on the variety that you buy, sage can be an annual or perennial. It grows well in sunshine and has beautiful purple flowers. The leaves are easy to pick and dry (to use for later).

Strawberries – Perennial plants which love good soil, sun and water. When they are happy, they'll grow like weeds and take over your garden which can mean a lot of juicy strawberries. They typically bear fruit earlier in the summer.

Green Beans and Peas – Perennial plants which can be started by putting seeds in the ground in the spring (when depends on where you're located and the type of bean). The pole varieties will climb string and lattice while the bush varieties will grow into short bushes. Fun for kids to pick and easy to maintain, green beans and pea varieties (like snap and snow peas) don't require a ton of space.

Swiss chard – A gorgeous annual plant that has thick stalks (some varieties are brightly colored in yellow and pink) with gorgeous big dark leaves. This plant will generally grow the entire summer and looks wonderful in a flower garden. Aside from watering it, all you have to do is pick off (and cook) the stalks around the outside of the plant as they mature.

Lettuce – An annual plant that does not like the heat, lettuce is fairly easy to grow. Follow the growing instructions and before you know it, you'll have heads of lettuce to enjoy.

Kale & Collard Greens – Annual plants that are incredibly hardy, easy to grow and can tolerate big differences in temperature. These two plants require more space than the rest on this list as they can get fairly large.

If you don't have a green thumb (as I didn't either in the beginning), pick a few plants and give things a try. You'll never learn how to garden unless you get in there and experiment. At first my garden didn't thrive, but with time, experience and some research, I figured out what I personally can and can't grow.

Start with herbs if you're nervous and remember… no one is stuck with a "brown thumb". If you are determined to start growing some of your own food, there are plenty of resources in your community and online to help you get started. Also, ask for help from those whom you already know are successful gardeners. Most gardeners I know love to talk about what has worked for them and share their best growing tips.

CHAPTER 14

NUTS, SEEDS, AVOCADOS & COCONUT

I LOVE NUTS, SEEDS AND COCONUT because they add great flavor to food and can serve as nutritious snacks in between meals. However, I've found that most people have no idea how to keep them fresh. The bigger concern is dealing with the nuts and seeds since they can either be purchased raw or roasted.

HOW TO KEEP NUTS & SEEDS LONGER

Generally, roasted nuts and seeds can be stored in airtight containers away from light. The same goes for nuts and seeds still in their shells which protects them from going bad.

If you purchase raw, hulled (or de-shelled) nuts and seeds, they must be stored in the refrigerator or freezer. Raw nuts and seeds which no longer have their shell go bad much faster and become rancid as the fat comes into contact with air and light. Should you see any areas of raw nuts become darkened or black, they've gone bad.

Also, know that nuts and seeds cannot last forever. If you can't remember when you purchased whatever you've got left in your home, it's probably best to toss them. I try not to keep nuts around for longer than three to four months in the fridge.

On any given day of the week, you can find the following nuts and seeds in my freezer:

- **Raw Hulled Nuts** – Walnuts, Pecans, Pine Nuts, Almonds, Macadamia
- **Raw Hulled Seeds** – Sunflower, Pepita (Pumpkin Seeds), Sesame

I keep a variety on hand so that I can use them to top salads, gluten-free grain dishes, add to recipes or eat as snacks. I also use the almonds to make my own almond milk. My recipe can be found in Chapter 19.

HOW TO STORE COCONUT

Similar to nuts and seeds, raw coconut is stored in airtight containers in the freezer or fridge while toasted coconut would be kept in the kitchen cabinet. Coconut doesn't quite have the same sense of urgency in going bad as that of nuts and seeds. Coconut butter and oil are kept away from light in airtight containers. They can withstand the fluctuation in temperature throughout the year and will naturally go from solid to liquid as the weather shifts from cold to hot.

I love to cook with coconut milk (the fat from the coconut that you can generally purchase in a can from the ethnic food aisle), however I've found that a large percentage ends up going bad sooner than I can use an entire can. My solution to this problem is to freeze unused portions of the coconut milk in ice cube trays. Once frozen, store the coconut milk ice cubes in freezer bags to add to recipes or even smoothies.

A more cost effective way to get coconut milk is to make it yourself. A single can of organic coconut milk can cost $3 and up, however if you have a Vitamix® or a high-powered food processor, you can make as much as you want for a tiny fraction of the price. Plus, you can control the ingredients and keep it very basic.

One point I want to share is that the coconut milk sold in cartons as a dairy alternative is not the same at the coconut milk I'm referencing here. The dairy alternative is highly processed to act very similar to cow's milk or other vegan milks on the market. You could use the coconut milk recipe here in place of dairy in recipes, however it has a much higher fat content.

MAKE YOUR OWN COCONUT MILK (FAT)

Add ½ cup of unsweetened, raw shredded coconut to your Vitamix® with two cups of water. Blend on high for three minutes. That's it!

Store this just as you would the leftovers of a purchased can. If you decide to keep some of it in the fridge, you may need to shake it up a bit due to natural settling.

HOW TO KEEP AVOCADOS LONGER

One of the most frequent questions I get from clients is about how to make the second half of an avocado last longer. Avocados can be very expensive depending on where you live, what time of year it is and if you have access to them where you live.

GF SAVVY TIP
To ripen avocados faster, place them in a fruit bowl (or a paper bag for even faster results) with bananas and apples. Natural gases from the fruit will speed up the rate of ripening.

I learned from a friend who is originally from Oaxaca, Mexico that the trick to keeping the flesh of an avocado from turning so quickly is the pit. An avocado is predominately made of healthy fat which begins to oxidize when it's exposed to air. The pit slows down this process and can extend the life of that second half of avocado for days after you've eaten the first.

When cutting open an avocado, **cut lengthwise around the pit**. Then grab each half of the avocado in your hands and gently twist (or crack) apart the halves from the pit which will stay lodged in one half. Cut first from the half of the avocado that does not have the pit attached. If you do not use the entire half, place it back on top of the pit and then keep it in the fridge.

If you do use the entire half, place the half with the pit in the fridge. There's honestly no need to wrap it up with foil or place it in a zipper-lock bag or container. When you're ready to eat it (within a few days of cutting the avocado open), remove the pit by wedging a sharp knife in the pit and turning it to break its seal with the rest of the avocado flesh. The top layer may get dried out, but you can easily skim it off with a knife and eat the green flesh underneath.

GF SAVVY TIP

If you buy too many avocados and they ripen at the same time, you can freeze the pureed flesh in airtight containers in the freezer. Make sure to remove air bubbles by pressing the contents into the container and smoothing out the top layer.

CHAPTER 15:
HELPFUL KITCHEN TOOLS

K ITCHEN TOOLS ARE IMPORTANT and can make your cooking life easier and a heck of a lot less stressful. Perhaps you already have some of these devices in your kitchen, so take an inventory of what you have before going to buy all new tools. And remember, if you're not used to using a particular kitchen device, you will become comfortable with practice and repetition.

This is my recommended list of go-to kitchen tools that I use on a weekly basis. All kitchen items listed here can be found at most department stores, kitchen supply stores, and superstores. Like anything, you get what you pay for. Do your homework, compare brands, read reviews, and ask for recommendations!

KITCHEN KNIVES

Good knives are a must as well as the number one kitchen tool I recommend. You don't need a whole knife set. Focus on purchasing only one or two to get started.

These two knives are a great place to start, and may be all you need:

- **Chef's knife:** A good chef's knife will make chopping and prepping food so much more enjoyable. It is used for most cutting chores like slicing, chopping, dicing, mincing, julienne cuts, disjointing large cuts of meat, smashing garlic, and more.

- **Paring knife:** For small intricate work like peeling and coring, a paring knife is your best solution. A good paring knife usually measures between 3 to 5 inches long. It is ideal for mincing herbs and garlic or coring strawberries, tomatoes, apples, pears, etc. The short pointed blade gives a paring knife precision and versatility.

Good quality kitchen knives are not cheap, but truly is an investment that can last a lifetime. Between the two suggested, the main one to get first is the Chef's Knife. I use mine nearly every other day and am eternally grateful for how easy it makes chopping and cutting.

If cost is an issue, there are a few ways to make this type of investment that will probably cost you between $100 to $200. Since these knives are found at most stores, you could request gift cards from friends and family to reduce your financial burden. You could also add them to your birthday, wedding or holiday wish list. Or you may be able to find some secondhand.

When looking for a quality knife, be certain it is sturdy and balanced with the blade (also called the "tang") running the entire length of the knife. This means that the metal will go from the pointy tip all the way through the entire butt of the handle for added stability and better control. I personally use knives from WÜSTHOF®.

To keep your knives working for years to come, proper care is key. Here are a few tips to keeping your kitchen knives in proper working order:

- **Avoid the dishwasher.** The dishwasher will make your knives dull. Carefully hand-wash kitchen knives in warm soapy water and dry them thoroughly before putting them away.
- **Protect the blade when in storage.** A knife's blade dulls each time it is rubbed against another object, especially metal. Store your kitchen knives in a utensil drawer with a protective blade sleeve, in a wooden knife block, or on a wall-mounted magnetic strip.
- **Use only wooden cutting boards.** Cutting on plastic, bam-

boo, and stone boards will dull your knives. Maple is best and will last a lifetime, but any wooden cutting board will do. (NOTE: Because gluten can easily contaminate wooden cutting boards, buy a brand new wooden cutting board if you have not done so already that will only be used for gluten-free food.)

- **Sharpen each year by a professional.** A very sharp knife is safer to use than a dull one. You can also purchase knife sharpening kits which can help keep them running for quick tune-ups throughout the year.

SLOW COOKER

The slow cooker is the second most important kitchen tool for healthy eating on a budget. I personally can't live without mine.

People often refer to this tool as a Crock-Pot®, which is actually a brand name.

A slow cooker is a countertop electrical cooking appliance that is used for simmering, which requires maintaining a relatively low temperature, allowing unattended cooking for many hours. For example, I often make a large pot of chicken soup in my slow cooker. It takes about ten minutes to get everything together and then it cooks overnight while I sleep. In the morning, the food is ready to eat or pack and take to work.

Buying, operating, and cooking with a slow cooker is very savvy. Slow cookers cost between $30 to $100 and can save you hundreds over purchasing fancy countertop convection toaster ovens and broilers.

How a slow cooker saves you time

Cook entire meals with multiple servings while you sleep or are at work.

Spend less time in front of your stove trying to get food on the table.

Use frozen vegetables and tougher cuts of meat that require long cooking times that all create great meals once it's done.

How a slow cooker saves you money

A slow cooker can cut your grocery bill significantly by allowing you to buy cheaper cuts of meat and tenderizing them over low heat for a longer time.

Vegetarians can also cut their grocery bills by using a slow cooker to soak and cook dried beans, instead of buying the canned variety.

Cooking with a slow cooker saves energy compared to using an oven.

Finally, you save money by using your slow cooker to make large quantities of food with enough for leftovers.

What model slow cooker do I buy?

There are many brands, models, and sizes to choose from. You can spend $20 to $100 or more on a slow cooker. Sizes range from 1.5 quarts (for dips) to seven quarts or more.

Here is a list of a few slow cooker manufacturers available in the United States (in alphabetical order).

- All-Clad®
- Breville®
- Crock-Pot®
- Cuisinart®
- De'Longhi®
- Hamilton Beach®
- KitchenAid®
- Proctor Silex®
- VitaClay®
- West Bend®

You do not need to get a high-end fancy digital model with all sorts of buttons and options. In my experience, models with high-end options tend to break easier than simpler models. Find a model that fits your needs and budget. I suggest choosing a larger size over the fancy features.

However, if you are wondering which features to select, these two are worth the expense:

- **Digital Timer:** The *Timer* option allows you to set the cook time (usually six hours on HIGH and four hours on LOW) and leave. The slow cooker will turn off (or Keep Warm) even if you're not there.
- **Removable stoneware:** Having the option to take out the ceramic crock (the receptacle where you put the food) is practical. First, it makes cleaning easier. Second, it allows you to prepare food the night before, keep it in the refrigerator and place it in the machine in the morning.

Read reviews, ask friends, and do research to choose the right model for you. You will not regret it.

What do I cook in a slow cooker?

Soups, stews, chili, entire chickens, tougher cuts of meat, casseroles, and other main course dishes are all possible using a slow cooker. Your food cooks while you sleep or are at work. As I said before - you do not need to get a fancy model loaded with electronics. Mine only has a knob with "Off", "Keep Warm", "Low," and "High."

How long should I cook it for?

Most dishes benefit from a slow, gentle heat to bring out the flavors, so use the "low" setting as often as possible. This also means you don't need to worry if you're heading out of the house for the day.

As a general rule of thumb, if a dish usually takes:

- 15 to 30 minutes to cook: Slow cook one to two hours on high, four to six hours on low
- 30 minutes to one hour to cook: Slow cook two to three hours on high, five to seven hours on low
- One to two hours to cook: Slow cook three to four hours on high, six to eight hours on low
- Two to four hours to cook: Slow cook four to six hours on high, eight to twelve hours on low

Root vegetables, like carrots and beets, can take longer than meat and other vegetables, so put these at the bottom of the pot.

OVEN

Just about every kitchen has an oven! It's not just a spot to permanently store pots and pans—it's also a great way to make several batches of food on four trays (or more depending on how many racks you have) at the same time. For example, place a tray of vegetables on one rack, and another with meat, all roasting at the same time which you can then save and eat throughout the week.

Use baking sheets to roast vegetables, meat, whole sweet potatoes, casseroles, meatloaves, and any other dishes that will provide multiple servings.

RICE COOKER

A standard rice cooker is designed to bring rice (and other grains like quinoa) to a boil, sense when it needs to reduce to a simmer, then lower the heat again to keep rice at serving temperature without overcooking it.

Rice cookers make it easy to cook grains while you prepare the rest of your meal. Simply add rice (or other grains), water, set it, and walk away. You do not have to pay attention to it at all. The rice cooker will thoroughly cook its contents and stop when the grains are done.

For as little as $16, you can buy a rice cooker at any store that sells simple kitchen appliances. A rice cooker is simple enough to use that your spouse or children can help out in the kitchen.

What's more, a rice cooker with additional controls can cook more than just rice and quinoa! Here are other foods that can be prepared in an electric rice cooker:

- Oats
- Vegetables
- Fish
- Meat
- Beans
- Risotto (without stirring)
- Poached fruit

Rice cookers usually come with a steaming basket that is placed on top to cook vegetables, fish, or meat while the grains cook.

PRESSURE COOKER

While not an essential, I know some people who swear by their pressure cooker.

A pressure cooker is a sealed vessel that does not permit air or liquids to escape below a pre-set pressure. Use a pressure cooker to cook food more quickly than conventional cooking methods while saving time and energy. Pressure cooking can be used to quickly simulate the effects of long braising or simmering.

To understand how a pressure cooker works, the pressure is initially created by boiling cooking liquid (like water or broth) inside a sealed pressure cooker. The trapped steam increases the internal pressure and temperature. Afterwards, the pressure is slowly released so that the vessel can be safely opened.

Almost any food that can be cooked in steam or water-based liquids can be cooked in a pressure cooker.

It is important to read the instruction manual before use. Most instruction manuals contain recipes and general cooking instructions (like cooking times and how much liquid to add).

ELECTRIC SPICE (OR COFFEE) GRINDER

A spice or coffee grinder is another great and inexpensive gadget to have on hand so that you can buy spices in their whole form, which will last longer than if you buy them pre-ground. Read more about this in Chapter 10.

BLENDER, FOOD PROCESSOR & IMMERSION BLENDER

While these three items are different, they do have some similarities. Budget and cooking needs will determine which of these tools you will want to purchase. There are price ranges for all budgets, so you will find something to fit your needs. Again, you get what you pay for—less expensive models may not last as long or be as powerful as more expensive, sturdier brands.

High Powered Blender

Though standard blenders are fine, high-powered blenders offer a wide variety of options.

Vitamix® and Blendtec® are the best high-end, high-powered options out there. Because they are quite pricey, they are a perfect item to add to a gift or wedding registry or birthday/holiday wish list. You can also save money by purchasing used or refurbished models.

There are many lower grade blenders to choose from that are quite affordable. However, keep in mind that high-end blenders have a ton of horse power which can easily create soups (and can get them to become hot), nut milks, butters, homemade ice cream, smooth smoothies, sauces, and so much more. You actually save money in the long run by making your own milks, butters, and smoothies compared to purchasing them ready-made.

When investing in one, get a model that offers a variable speed control knob.

Food Processor

A food processor comes in handy when shredding or slicing in large quantities of hard-to-handle foods, like carrots and cabbage. A food processor can also chop items that a blender does not handle very well.

Immersion Blender

This small handy tool allows you to blend and completely purée soups and stews. You can also do the same by using a blender or food processor in batches.

Toaster Oven

This is not what I would call a must-have gadget, but it definitely has its place in a budget-conscious kitchen. A toaster oven is like having a miniature version of an oven. It can be used to bake, toast, broil, and roast meat, fish, and certain veggies.

Because it is smaller, it takes up less space and uses less energy to cook your food. This also means you can't cook in bulk like you can in a regular oven. But it comes in handy when cooking for one or two.

Place the broiler tray INSIDE while the oven preheats, which allows the food to cook much faster because it is cooking from both the top and bottom.

CHAPTER 16:

GLUTEN-FREE MEAL PLANNING ON A BUDGET

NOW THAT YOU HAVE all the nitty-gritty information on what to buy, you need to know how to put it all together. If not, it's just a lot of food stored in your home that probably will not get used because it's so easy to forget what you have on hand.

Before we jump in, I want to share a quote with you that a client of mine has repeated to me many times over. He's a basketball coach and has run several very successful businesses. I take what he has to say seriously because I know that it's coming from real life experience.

"Failing to prepare is preparing to fail."

Though you've probably heard this commonly used quote before, it rings especially true with food and meal planning. If you don't make a plan, you will fail in some way, shape, or form. Food will go bad or be wasted, which ultimately means wasted money. Nobody likes that.

As I shared in the Preface to the book, a family of four in America wastes up to 25 percent of their food during the course of a year. This also means that 25 percent of the money spent on food is wasted which can total **around $2,700 for a normal non-gluten-free diet**. That amount gets supersized to approximately $5,500 once we add in the fact that the gluten-free diet is 242 percent more expensive. Utilizing meal planning to avoid waste and using some of the tricks I've shared in this book thus far doesn't sound so bad now, right? Think of how much money you could be saving!

By creating some structure around weekly meal planning, you can eliminate excess stress, save money, and ultimately get creative with food. It allows you the peace of mind to worry less and enjoy your life more because you won't be fixated on what you will be making for dinner every night. Lunch will be ready for you to grab each morning, and breakfast may be as simple as blending up a smoothie or reheating something made the previous day.

Though this might not fit the traditional definition of "fast food," it is still fast and convenient. Plus, it's homemade with your own loving hands, which know better than anyone else that what was made is safe for you to eat.

HOW TO GET STARTED

The first piece to start planning on a budget is to know that **making leftovers are key to cooking less and saving money**. Those unwilling to eat leftovers will be doomed to cooking much more than those who are comfortable reheating food. By considering how many extra servings of food you can make in one cooking session, it will dramatically increase the number of meals you will have prepared as well as what you'll be able to stockpile in your freezer for later.

Secondly, make an agreement with yourself to **cook two or three times each week**. Review your weekly calendar to determine what days and times you will be able to devote to cooking. Mark down these days and times for yourself. These specific time blocks for cooking must be taken into account when you plan out your week.

One of the days you will cook should be what I like to call a "Big Cooking Day". Mine is Sunday because I have more time to go to the market and prepare much of what I will need for the rest of the week. As discussed in previous chapters, you want to do as much of the chopping, dicing, and cooking as makes sense on this day.

The day or so prior should be your time to plan. Initially this phase may take you more time, but as you get into the swing of things, it will become faster as you add more recipes into your repertoire and become more comfortable. Planning includes picking the recipes you'll cook for the week, laying out the recipes on a grid or list that will make sense for you, creating a shopping list, and developing the action steps for each day that will take the worry out of the process.

Have you ever bought all the ingredients for a meal at the store and on the day you intended to make dinner, arrived home at 5:30pm to realize that you forgot to defrost the meat? Frustrated, you decide to go buy dinner because it would take too long otherwise. It is my belief that dinner should never take more than 30 minutes or so to get on the table. By preparing in advance and knowing that you needed to set the meat (in this particular case) out to defrost while you're at work, you have a greater chance for success.

Grocery shopping can happen on the day you create your weekly food plan, the day before cooking or on your "Big Cooking Day". I prefer to grocery shop the day before I cook so it's less that I have to do on Sunday.

Lastly, pick one or two other nights during your work week where you can afford to cook a 30 minute meal or put something together in the slow cooker, for example.

Here is a peek inside my meal planning process so that you can see it more clearly:

Saturday: Create food plan and grocery list. Go grocery shopping.

Sunday: Big Cooking Day! Cook several different recipes and prep parts of meals for the week.

Tuesday night: Cook 30-minute meal.

Wednesday night: Put slow cooker recipe together to cook overnight.

I also allow for one night a week where I will be eating out of the house. If you eat out more often, keep that in mind when you make your plan.

CREATING YOUR FOOD PLAN

I find that meal planning is much easier when you ask others in your household what they are interested in eating for that week. This will make the process of cooking and eating more harmonious within your family. It may even open up a dialogue and get others actively engaged in the process, which reduces your own amount of work.

With a large, blank sheet of paper, jot down the recipes you would like to make for the coming week. Think about everything—breakfast, lunch, dinner, snacks, and even dessert. This is a brainstorming session, so don't edit yourself now. Recipes can always be removed and others added to the list as you see fit. I would suggest that you pick between 10 and 15 recipes for a complete menu plan for the week, however buying some pre-made sauces, meals and other items can reduce the number of recipes you'll actually need. If you focus on cooking large one-pot meals (like chili) which include lots of vegetables, you will be able to further reduce the amount of recipes.

Once your list is created, use the blank meal planning grid from the Companion Budget Menu Planning Packet (see the final page of this Chapter for details on how to download it) to plot out what you will eat for different meal blocks: Breakfast, AM Snack, Lunch, PM Snack, Dinner, and Dessert (optional). Mark off what meals will be eaten outside of the home so you don't have to worry about them. Start with your "Big Cooking Day" and circle what you intend on making. Then begin to plot out what the leftover meals will look like for the first few days.

It's important to note that what is cooked on Sunday will be eaten as part of Sunday lunch and dinner (two separate meals) and then reused for Monday's lunch and dinner, Tuesday lunch and dinner and perhaps Wednesday's lunch too. Keeping this in mind, you may find it best to cook extra servings (sometimes doubling a recipe) so that you have enough for everyone. Only you know how much everyone in your family eats, so you will need to be the judge of serving sizes.

Next, drop in the meals for the smaller cooking days (like a Wednesday night) and plot those out as well. Once you've laid out your meals and snacks, look to see what's missing. Maybe you need more veggies and a healthy gluten-free starch on Thursday to go with a pot roast. Now you can decide what should be added. In this case, because you might utilize your oven to cook the pot roast, it would make sense to roast a bunch of root vegetables along with some whole sweet potatoes.

Or perhaps you're making chili in your slow cooker on Tuesday overnight. You'd like to add in some greens, so have some baby spinach and frozen peas on hand to add to your pot once it's cooked in the morning. You could also consider quickly sautéing some greens that were prepped on Sunday and saved in the fridge. Adding a healthy fat such as avocado slices or guacamole makes the meal go further since fat is more calorically-dense than carbs and protein.

Cooking a large batch of rice or quinoa in the rice cooker takes two minutes to put together, cooks on its own, and adds more food to the meal. To take this a step further, you may want to use the extra rice cooked in this example to add to a sautéed vegetable dish on Friday that will be paired with some roasted salmon.

Next, create a shopping list from your crafted menu. Make sure to denote the number of items you will need (the number of onions, for example) if multiple recipes call for them.

Finally, look through your list starting with your "Big Cooking Day" (for this example, we will assume it's Sunday) and start jotting down what recipes will be made for Sunday. Then create a subsection beneath the menu grid called "Prepping." Scan through the week and the recipe list and see what you could do on Sunday that would make your life easier during the week. Maybe it's chopping up all the veggies or roasting sweet potatoes that will be reheated for later. Either way, write every detail down so you don't have to remember to do it.

Mark down the other days of the week, and if there are any relevant details that you will need to remember to help expedite the cooking process, create an Action List and write it down. Do not leave anything to your memory. I don't say this to imply that you are forgetful or absent-minded. I know that life happens and often our good intentions can get fumbled when things do not go as planned. By writing down all the things you have to remember, you free your brain up to be more present and focused.

For example, if you've got to defrost the meat for your slow cooker on Wednesday night, make a note on Wednesday that says "AM - Pull meat out to defrost."

The bottom line is that this process allows you to stop expending so much time, energy, and money struggling to cook healthy gluten-free food. Instead, **you can be on autopilot during the week**, simply following the focused plan you created earlier.

To make this process easier:

- Download the **Companion Budget Menu Planning Packet** (see the final page of this Chapter for details on how to do so)
- Buy an erasable meal planning grid with erasable markers
- Use a small notepad to keep track of the leftovers and important staples in the freezer
- Hang your weekly prepping notes on the fridge
- Put all the recipes together that you'll need in one spot for easy access

YOUR "BIG COOKING DAY"

Whatever day works for you to cook, make meals that can be refrigerated for a few days. Fish and seafood do not fall into this category. I usually only make them when I know that I won't need several of days' worth of food to eat without cooking again, as they really only hold up for about a day after cooking.

My goal is to utilize as much of my kitchen as possible. The rice cooker is making a big batch of rice for the next few days plus some to freeze for later. The oven is packed with meat, veggies, and sweet potatoes. My slow cooker may be making a soup or else one is simmering on the stove top.

I also look at my Action List to see what I can prepare in advance. Perhaps onions need to be chopped or garlic minced. Or maybe I'm getting my snacks ready and prepared for the week in individual baggies or containers. Whatever it is, I do what I can on my "Big Cooking Day" because I know that during the week it may not happen.

A NOTE ABOUT LEFTOVERS

I always suggest to clients to make extra food for imaginary members of their family. Before sitting down to a meal, add these additional servings to freezer bags or containers to put in the freezer for later. Creating a stockpile of pre-cooked food can be a lifesaver if something comes up unexpectedly or you don't have as much time during a particular week to cook.

Also, if you are planning on using what you've cooked for lunches, make sure to create these lunch meals before sitting down to a meal. This will help family members from overeating (too often we go back for seconds and thirds because we see more food on the table that really should be saved for later). And it will mean that you've taken care of your needs for the following days before you eat, become tired, and want to relax.

If for some reason, you have extra portions lingering after a few days and you know your next cooking day is coming up, put them into a container or freezer bag and store them in your freezer for another time.

Download your *complimentary* Companion Budget Menu Planning Packet!!

VISIT:
www.glutenfreeschool.com/members/4rt8fg965tf/

Enter your email address and click Submit. Then go to your email box, open the email titled "Response Required" and click the link inside of the email to confirm your email address.

Once you have confirmed your email, you will receive another email from me that will provide you the link to download your complimentary Companion Budget Menu Planning Packet which includes sample meal plans (so you can see how it's done), blank menu plans to use as well as other extras to shorten the learning curve!

CHAPTER 17

GLUTEN-FREE SNACKING
ON A BUDGET

SOME OF THE WORST gluten-free snacks out there are pre-packaged. Plus, they are more costly long-term. What may seem "cheap" in the moment can add up quickly if you spend the time to do the math. Also, many are not good for your health as they rely on high glycemic starchy carbs and are loaded with sugar.

Truthfully, ANYTHING can be a snack. Leftovers can be a snack. You don't need to have something that looks like a "snack food" to qualify it as a snack. That said, your tastes and individual needs are entirely personal and it takes time to break away from old habits and mindset.

I generally advise clients to stick with lower glycemic fruits like apples, pears, grapefruit, and berries with some sort of healthy protein and fat options like guacamole, hummus and other bean dips, and nut butters. Hard-boiled eggs are a great snack as are vegetable sticks along with these dip options.

Here are 12 snack ideas that might help you break out of old not-so-healthy habits:

1. Apple with nut butter
2. Assorted berries or a pear with nuts
3. Yogurt with toasted, chopped nuts and berries
4. Small smoothie

5. 1 square of 72% (or higher) dark chocolate and nuts
6. Lettuce wraps with roasted meat and avocado slices
7. Small omelette with veggies
8. Hard-boiled egg with fresh cut veggies and hummus
9. ½ grapefruit with roasted sunflower seeds
10. Tea with almond milk and stevia
11. Celery sticks with nut butter
12. Grilled veggies with hummus and pesto drizzled on top

CHAPTER 18:

FINAL THOUGHTS

B Y CREATING A PLAN, sticking to it, and breaking out of old
food habits, you can easily save yourself time, money, and
your own personal sanity. I've demonstrated that cooking
every day isn't necessary and can save you in cases of an incredibly
hectic week or when an emergency arises. As an example, I had
a client whose mother became incredibly ill. For a week, she was
at the hospital every day visiting her for as long as she could stay.
Though her meal planning went out the window for these seven
days, she said it was the stockpile of food and the ways I showed
her to get food on the table quickly that saved her.

Every plan creates the space you want and need in your life to do
other things like enjoy your family and relax. Your mind won't
be so burdened and scattered. Living gluten-free takes a clear and
conscious choice to take care of yourself. Though initially it can
seem inconvenient, it doesn't have to be. Food does not have to
require so much time and money to taste good and be healthy.

If I could eat gluten-free on a tight budget, so can you no matter
what your financial circumstance. I've taught many of my clients
over the years these tricks to cooking faster, eating better, and ultimately feeling more like how you think you should. In time, it will
become second nature just like riding a bike. You will develop your
own repertoire of recipes (think of it as a personal cookbook), you
will know how to put all the pieces together, and you will have the
peace of mind knowing that you have safe, gluten-free "fast food"
waiting for you in the freezer.

One final thought—to simplify the food preparing process in your home, get your kids and spouse involved to take off some of the added time and pressure of having to do everything yourself. Some of these kitchen devices are incredibly simple to operate (like a rice cooker). Plus it gets your family involved and caring about food and nutrition. Their enthusiasm can be very helpful to keep you going should you ever get caught in a cooking rut.

I hope that you will find this book to be an invaluable resource to jumpstart your own process of not only saving money, but eating healthier, safe, gluten-free food. Even if you implement a few of these tips each week, you will soon notice a difference. Please stop by at GlutenFreeSchool.com and let me know what tips you've found most helpful as well as any creative solutions you've discovered along the way. I wish you the best of luck on your gluten-free journey!

CHAPTER 19

GLUTEN-FREE STARTER RECIPES

ALL RECIPES IN THIS BOOK are gluten-free, soy-free, and corn-free. I have marked each recipe with additional labels to note if the recipe is Vegan, Vegetarian, Paleo, Dairy-free, Egg-free and/or Nut-free.

RECIPE LISTING

Almond Milk

Sausage & Veggies

Poached Egg

Baked Mediterranean Eggs

Brown Rice Porridge

Chopped Veggie Salad

Green Salad

Easy Guacamole

Red Lentil Soup

Crockpot Chicken Soup

Crockpot Sausage Soup

Quick Black Bean Soup

Quick Root Veggie Soup

Creamy Asparagus Soup

Spicy Chorizo Chili

Herb-Roasted Chicken & Baby Carrots

Pan-Browned Chicken

Turkey Meatloaf

Roasted Brussels Sprouts

Spicy Sweet Potato Wedges

Roasted Beets

Roasted Cherry Tomatoes & Beans

Squash & Peas

Mexican Fried Rice

Quick Apple Crisp

Brown Rice Pudding

Healthy Fruity Freezer Pops

ALMOND MILK

Dairy-free / Vegan / Paleo / Egg-free
Serves 4 to 6

- 1 cup raw almonds, soaked for 8 to 12 hours in cool water
- 4 cups cold water

GF SAVVY TIP

*To make this recipe, a high-speed blender such as a Vitamix® or Blendtec® works best. You may also want to use a **Nut Milk Bag** to strain out the almond pulp though it is not necessary. Unstrained almond milk is completely drinkable, but it will be thicker.*

To soak your almonds, measure them out and add water that covers them by 1 or 2 inches. Cover the container and place in the fridge to soak.

When you're ready to make your almond milk, discard soaking water and rinse almonds very well. Place them in your blender. Add 2 cups of water and begin to purée on the highest speed possible for 1 to 2 minutes, or until you see that everything has become pulverized.

Turn machine off, add remaining 2 cups of water, and blend on HIGH again for a minute or so. Then shut off again. You will see that a lot of foam has formed on the top of the milk. That's normal.

Wash your hands well and run the almond milk through your Nut Milk Bag. I like to do this in 3 or 4 batches because the pulp will run into the bag and you will need to squeeze the bag to get the excess milk out. I will usually squeeze the milk into a tempered glass measuring cup and then pour it into a mason jar.

Once finished, store in the fridge with the lid on. I've found my almond milk can stay just fine for 4 or 5 days in the fridge. Note that it will begin to separate a bit, so just shake up the jar before you use it.

As for the pulp, you can either toss it or dehydrate it and use it as almond flour.

SAUSAGE (OR EGGPLANT) & VEGGIES

Paleo with additional Vegetarian & Vegan options** / Dairy-free / Nut-free
Serves 1

- 1 large sausage link (pork, chicken or beef) **
- ¾ cup onions, sliced into half moons
- 2 to 3 handfuls baby spinach
- ¾ cup zucchini or yellow squash, chopped
- Garlic powder
- Sea salt
- Black pepper
- 1 to 2 tablespoons extra virgin olive oil
- 1 cage-free, organic egg, scrambled with vegetables (optional)

Heat oil in pan over medium heat. When it is fluid in the pan, add onions and sauté until they become translucent.

Add sausage and allow to cook for about 3 to 4 minutes, flipping as necessary (cook less if the sausage is pre-cooked).

Add zucchini or squash and sauté the entire dish together for another 3 to 4 minutes. As the sausage is fully cooked, add in the spinach with 1 to 2 tablespoons of water.

Keep everything moving and once the spinach has wilted, remove from heat and add a light dusting of garlic powder, a bit of sea salt, and black pepper, to taste.

Must be eaten by the following day.

** Vegetarian and Vegan options: Use ½ a small eggplant in place of sausage.

POACHED EGG

Vegetarian / Paleo / Dairy-free / Nut-free
Serves 1

- 1 organic egg
- 1 to 2 teaspoons brown rice vinegar
- Sea salt
- Black pepper

Gently crack open the egg in a small bowl and discard the shell.

In a small pot, bring water that is deep enough for the egg to sit in (3 or 4 inches high) to a near boil. As the water begins to boil, turn the heat down so that it is at a nice simmer.

Add vinegar and gently slide the egg into the water. As it begins to cook, use a slotted spoon to keep the egg from sticking to the bottom of the pan and to gently keep the egg white cooking near the egg yolk. Continue to cook for another 4 to 6 minutes depending on how well done you want your egg yolk. Remove egg from water and season to taste.

GF SAVVY TIP

Cook more than one egg at a time in the pan and store in the refrigerator for later use (such as over a salad later that day).

Consume by the end of the day.

BAKED MEDITERRANEAN EGGS

Vegetarian / Paleo / Dairy-free / Nut-free
Serves 2

- 2 medium ceramic ramekins
- 4 eggs
- 1 tablespoon red onion, finely chopped
- 2 tablespoons roasted red pepper, sliced
- 6 Kalamata olives, pitted and sliced
- ¼ cup baby spinach, thinly sliced
- A few fresh basil leaves, thinly sliced

Preheat oven to 400°F. Either oil the insides of the ramekins with a paper towel moistened with olive oil or spray the inside with olive oil spray. Divide the onions, roasted red pepper, and olives evenly in the bottoms of the ramekins. Place the spinach on top.

Crack the eggs and put two eggs in each ramekin, over top of the spinach. Add a pinch of salt and pepper and sprinkle with the fresh basil leaves. Cover the ramekins with foil and bake for 15 minutes, or until the eggs are cooked to your taste (less time for slightly runny; more time for firmer). Periodically lift the foil and jiggle the ramekin to check solidity of the egg.

When you are happy with egg consistency, remove from oven. Run a knife around the inside edge of the ramekin and turn upside down on a platter. Enjoy the beautiful colors!

Eat within a day or two of baking.

BROWN RICE PORRIDGE

Vegetarian / Vegan / Dairy-free / Egg-free
Serves 4 to 6

- 1 cup brown rice, rinsed
- 5 to 6 cups water (I personally use 5 cups)
- 2 large Granny Smith apples or 1 large Gala apple (sweeter), cored and cubed
- ¼ cup raisins
- ¼ cup shredded coconut
- ¼ teaspoon cinnamon
- ½ teaspoon pumpkin pie spice
- Pinch of sea salt

Optional ingredients
- 1 tablespoon organic creamy peanut butter or other nut butter (no salt and no sugar added)
- Stevia
- 1 tablespoon ground flax
- ½ serving of protein powder

Combine rice, water, apple, raisins, coconut, cinnamon, pumpkin pie spice, and salt in a slow cooker. Set to cook on low overnight, or about 8 hours. Wake up to a delicious smelling house and several days' worth of an awesome breakfast. Serve yourself some in a bowl, adjust spices, and stir in other optional items to taste such as peanut (or other nut) butter, protein powder, sweetener, and ground flax.

Lasts four or five days in fridge.

CHOPPED VEGGIE SALAD

Vegetarian / Vegan / Egg-free / Dairy-free / Nut-free / Paleo option**
Serves 4

- 1 bag baby spinach
- 1 cup fresh green beans, snapped into 2- or 3-inch pieces
- 2 large carrots, chopped
- Handful cherry tomatoes, halved
- 1 cucumber, chopped
- ½ small red onion, diced
- 1 zucchini, chopped
- 1 yellow squash, chopped
- ½ cup beans of choice, rinsed well**

Dressing:

- 3 tablespoons fresh chives, minced
- ¼ cup fresh lemon juice
- 1 tablespoon extra virgin olive oil
- Stevia to taste**
- 1 teaspoon fresh garlic, minced

If serving immediately, mix all ingredients in a bowl and serve.

If making ahead, mix dressing ingredients separately and pour over vegetables when ready to serve.

**Paleo option: Omit beans and add more green beans from salad. Omit stevia from dressing.

Lasts up to two days refrigerated.

GREEN SALAD

Vegetarian / Vegan / Paleo / Egg-free / Dairy-free / Nut-free
Serves 1

- 2 cups romaine lettuce, chopped or shredded
- 1 bulb of endive, washed and thinly sliced
- 1 avocado, cubed
- 1 pear, washed and cubed

Dressing:

- 1 tablespoon extra virgin olive oil
- 1 teaspoon raw red wine vinegar
- A few pinches of sea salt
- ½ teaspoon dried oregano
- 1 teaspoon rice vinegar (optional)

Combine greens, avocado, and pear in bowl.

Mix dressing ingredients separately, adjusting to taste, and pour over salad.

Must be eaten immediately.

QUICK VEGAN MEXICAN FRIED RICE

Vegan / Vegetarian / Dairy-free / Egg-free / Nut-free
Serves 4

- 3 tablespoons extra virgin olive oil
- 2 cups cooked brown rice
- 1 can black beans, drained and rinsed well
- 1 large tomato, chunked
- 1½ medium onions, sliced
- 3 cloves garlic, minced
- 1 cup frozen peas and carrot mix
- 2 tablespoons parsley, minced
- 1 teaspoon cumin seeds
- 1 teaspoon paprika
- 1 teaspoon chili powder
- ½ teaspoon turmeric
- 1 tablespoon sea salt
- Juice of half a lime (optional)

Add oil, cumin seeds, and half the amount of the paprika, chili powder, and turmeric to a sauté pan over medium heat. Keep the spices moving around the pan. Once they become fragrant and the oil is hot, add the onions and toss to coat them well. Sauté for a couple of minutes until they become transparent, then add in garlic and keep stirring the mixture for another minute or so.

Add in the rice, tomato, frozen veggies, and the rest of the spices along with the salt and combine well. Allow to simmer for about 3 to 5 more minutes, or until everything seems to thicken a bit. Then remove from heat and add beans and parsley.

For a nice added flavor enhancer, squeeze some fresh juice of a lime into your bowl. Enjoy!

Must be consumed within 4 days.

RED LENTIL SOUP

Vegetarian / Vegan / Egg-free / Dairy-free / Nut-free

Serves 6

- 1 pound yellow or orange lentils, rinsed thoroughly
- 1 can (28- or 32-ounce) diced tomatoes
- 3 large garlic cloves, minced
- 1 medium onion, chopped
- 5 cups water
- 3 tablespoons extra virgin olive oil
- 1 tablespoon sea salt
- 1 teaspoon black pepper
- 1 cup loosely packed fresh basil leaves
- 1 avocado, cubed (optional)

In a large pan, sauté onions and garlic for 4 to 5 minutes, until onions are translucent. Add the tomatoes and water and bring to a simmer.

Meanwhile in a separate pot, bring 4 cups water to a boil. Add lentils and reduce heat to a simmer. Any foam that rises to the top should be skimmed off with a large spoon and discarded. Cook lentils until they become tender, 10 to 15 minutes.

Once lentils are softened, add tomato mixture to lentils and season with salt and pepper, adjusting to taste. Loosely slice or tear up basil leaves and simmer for another 20 minutes. If soup is too thick, add water.

Garnish with cubed avocado if desired.

Lasts four days in fridge. Leftovers can be frozen up to three months.

CROCK POT CHICKEN SOUP
Dairy-free / Egg-free / Paleo-option**
Serves 6

- 6 chicken legs with skin and bones, rinsed
- 1 medium onion, diced
- 2 stalks celery, rinsed and chopped
- 3 large carrots, scrubbed and chopped
- Water
- ½ teaspoon ground black pepper
- 1 tablespoon sea salt
- 3 medium garlic cloves, minced (optional—only if you want a strong garlic flavor)

Place chicken and veggies in ceramic bowl of crock pot and add pepper. Fill up the bowl with water until you come to about ½ inch below the lip of the bowl.

Faster cooking: Start soup out on HIGH until it comes to a boil. Then turn down to LOW and cook for 4 to 6 hours or until vegetables are tender and chicken will fall off the bone.

Slower cooking (good for overnight or cooking while at work): Cook soup on LOW for 8 to 10 hours or until vegetables are tender and chicken will fall off the bone.

Then add salt to taste and adjust pepper as needed.

Remove chicken from soup and clean the meat off of the bones. Discard both the bones and skin. Store the meat in a separate container that doesn't have broth and vegetables in it.

Make individual soup bowls by adding some broth, vegetables and meat. Then add additional ingredients such as cooked rice or for the Paleo option**, add more veggies and greens. I love to get creative and top my soup with things that you might not initially think of like avocado chunks and pico de gallo.

You can also freeze some of the broth for 2 to 3 months. And for a different flavor profile, try subbing the 6 chicken legs for 2 turkey legs.

Lasts four days in fridge. Leftovers can be frozen up to three months.

SLOW-COOKER SAUSAGE SOUP

Dairy-free / Egg-free / Nut-free

Serves 6

- 3 to 4 long mild uncooked gluten-free sausages, cut into 1-inch slices
- 1 28-ounce can diced tomatoes
- 3 cups water
- 1 large sweet onion, diced
- 2 cups baby carrots
- 1 tablespoon fresh thyme
- 1 bay leaf
- 4 large garlic cloves, minced
- 1 teaspoon white pepper
- 1½ teaspoons sea salt
- 2 cans butter beans or white beans, rinsed well
- 1 cup frozen peas, defrosted (optional)

Add all ingredients except beans to a slow cooker. Cook on HIGH for 6 hours or on LOW for 8 to 9 hours.

Once the soup is cooked, add the butter beans (and peas if using), adjust seasonings, and serve!

Lasts four days in fridge. Leftovers can be frozen up to three months.

QUICK BLACK BEAN SOUP

Vegetarian / Vegan / Dairy-free / Egg-free / Nut-free
Serves 6

- 3 tablespoons extra virgin olive oil
- 1 medium onion, diced
- 2 garlic cloves, minced
- 1 red pepper, diced
- 1 teaspoon cumin
- 1 teaspoon chili powder
- 1 teaspoon paprika
- ½ teaspoon black pepper
- ¼ teaspoon turmeric
- ½ teaspoon oregano
- 5 cups water, divided
- 1½ teaspoons sea salt
- 3 cans low or no sodium black beans, rinsed thoroughly

In a deep sauté pan or pot, heat oil over medium heat. Add onions and cook for 3 minutes. Add garlic, red pepper, and spices and combine well.

Pour ½ cup water and keep everything moving in the pan as the red pepper softens, about 3 to 4 minutes.

Add beans and remaining water and cover. Once the mixture comes to a boil, remove from heat.

Either use an immersion blender (may still be gritty), a potato masher (will be rather chunky), or blend in batches (will render the smoothest consistency) to purée the soup to your liking. Adjust seasonings to taste and top with chunks of avocado.

Lasts four days in fridge. Leftovers can be frozen up to three months.

QUICK ROOT VEGGIE SOUP

Dairy-free / Egg-free / Nut-free / Vegan Option**
Serves 6

- 8 cups low or no sodium stock or broth (vegetable**, chicken, turkey, or beef)
- 1 cup wild rice
- 3 small to medium sweet potatoes, cubed with the skin on
- 1 medium onion, chunked
- 4 to 6 large garlic cloves, minced
- ½ bag of baby carrots
- 1 to 2 cans of beans, rinsed (black, pinto, black eyed peas, etc.)
- 1 cup frozen peas
- 1 tablespoon sea salt
- 1 teaspoon black pepper
- ¼ teaspoon (or less) cayenne pepper

In a large pot, bring broth or stock to a boil. Add vegetables (EXCEPT peas) and rice.

Once boiling again, turn down heat, cover, and simmer for 40 to 45 minutes, until carrots and sweet potatoes are soft. Then add beans, peas, and seasonings, adjusting to taste, and cook for another 5 minutes.

Lasts four days in fridge. Leftovers can be frozen up to three months.

CREAMY ASPARAGUS SOUP

*Paleo / Dairy-free / Egg-free / Nut-free / Vegan Option***
6 servings

- 6 cups low or no sodium stock or broth (vegetable**, chicken, turkey, or beef)
- 1 bunch asparagus, washed, trimmed, cut into 2-inch pieces
- 1 medium sweet onion, quartered
- 3 large garlic cloves, minced
- 1½ cups frozen peas
- 1 large sweet potato, pre-roasted or microwaved
- 3 tablespoons extra virgin olive oil
- ¼ teaspoon white pepper
- 1½ teaspoons sea salt
- Black pepper to taste
- Lemon wedges

Preheat oven to 425°F and line a baking sheet with foil or parchment. Heat stock or broth in a large pot. Once the liquid has come to a boil, add peas, turn down to a simmer, and cover.

In a separate bowl, add onions, garlic, olive oil, and asparagus, and mix until coated with oil. Lay vegetables on baking sheet and spread salt and pepper evenly over top. Keep this seasoning on the light side as you will adjust the final taste when everything is combined at the end. Put baking sheet in the oven for 12 minutes. Check every 4 to 6 minutes and move things around so the vegetables don't burn.

When vegetables are roasted, remove from oven and add them to the hot broth. Scoop out the flesh of the sweet potato and add to soup.

Purée the soup with an immersion blender or in batches in a blender or food processor.

Add the white pepper and the salt. Adjust seasonings to your liking.

When serving, squeeze fresh lemon juice over top.

Lasts four days in fridge. Leftovers can be frozen up to three months.

HERB-ROASTED CHICKEN & BABY CARROTS

Paleo / Dairy-free / Egg-free / Nut-free
4 servings

- 1 pound chicken pieces, boneless and skinless
- 1 bag baby carrots
- Extra virgin olive oil
- 1 teaspoon sea salt
- 1 teaspoon black pepper
- 1½ teaspoons fresh rosemary, minced
- 1 to 2 teaspoons garlic powder

Preheat oven to 425°F. Cover baking sheet with aluminum foil or parchment.

Rinse the chicken pieces and pat them dry, then place them along the outer sides of the baking sheet. Drizzle olive oil across chicken and brush the top of the chicken evenly with the oil. Sprinkle the chicken with ½ teaspoon rosemary and lightly coat with sea salt, pepper, and garlic powder.

In a bowl, combine baby carrots with 1 teaspoon salt, ½ teaspoon black pepper, 1 teaspoon rosemary, and 1 to 2 teaspoons garlic powder. Mix until carrots are well coated, then pour them into the middle of the baking sheet in a single layer.

Place sheet in oven and roast for 40 to 45 minutes. Turn the carrots after 20 minutes. Remove from oven, let sit for 5 minutes, then serve.

GF SAVVY TIP

For bulk cooking, use a separate baking sheet for the chicken and another for the carrots.

Lasts three to four days in the fridge.

PAN-BROWNED CHICKEN

Paleo / Dairy-free / Egg-free / Nut-free
Serves 2 to 4

- 4 chicken thighs with skin, deboned
- Sea salt
- Ground black pepper

Rinse and pat your chicken pieces dry. Evenly salt both sides of the chicken thighs.

Heat pan over medium and place each chicken thigh skin-side down. Allow to cook for about 15 to 18 minutes until skin is easily removable from pan surface thanks to the rendering fat. This is really important—do not try to pull the skin off of the pan. It will initially stick, but will release from the pan once it is almost ready to be flipped.

Once the skin is nicely browned, turn the chicken and cook for another 5 minutes to fully cook and lightly brown the underside.

Remove from heat and add black pepper to your liking.

Use chicken fat for a future use such as sautéing veggies or cooked grains for added flavor.

Lasts three days in fridge.

MOIST TURKEY MEATLOAF

Dairy-free / Egg-free / Nut-free

Serves 6

- 1 pound ground turkey
- 1 carrot
- 1 stalk celery
- 1 small onion
- 3 medium garlic cloves, minced
- 1½ teaspoons coconut palm sugar
- 1 cup gluten-free rolled oats
- 1½ egg replacer (see explanation below)
- ½ 3-ounce can tomato paste
- 1 teaspoon Dijon mustard
- 1 tablespoon balsamic vinegar
- 1½ teaspoons sea salt
- 1 tablespoon black pepper
- Pinch of cinnamon

Preheat oven to 350°F. The next best thing to do is to prepare the egg replacement. You can certainly use the powdered egg replacer (just follow the directions to equal about 1½ eggs) or use ground flaxseed to create a binder as follows: Mix 1½ tablespoons of ground flaxseed with 4½ tablespoons warm water. Allow to sit for a few minutes so that it can thicken after you've 'beat' it a bit with a fork.

Cut up the carrot, celery, garlic, and onion in chunks and use a food processor to mince/purée. If you have a small food processor, you will need to blend each vegetable by itself. Add each (and whatever liquid results) into a large mixing bowl. Add egg replacer, oats, sugar, tomato paste, mustard, vinegar, and spices. Combine everything and then add in the turkey meat and mix everything until it becomes a consistent mass.

Place turkey mixture in a baking container and smooth out top.

If using a metal pan, you may want to oil the pan before adding in the turkey mixture. If you use CorningWare® bakeware, you can just place the meat in the bowl (I've never had a problem with sticking once it has cooked). Smooth out the top and cover with foil, or ideally a lid if you have one that is made for whatever dish/pan you are using. Place on the middle rack and bake for about 35 minutes.

Then remove the lid or foil and bake for another 5 to 10 minutes. Once done, allow to cool for at least 5 minutes before serving to let everything settle into place.

Lasts four days in fridge. Leftovers can be frozen up to one month.

SPICY CHORIZO CHILI

Dairy-free / Egg-free / Nut-free
Serves 4 to 6

- 1 package gluten-free chorizo, casing sliced open to release meat
- 2 to 3 medium yellow squash, washed and chunked
- 1 large onion, chunked
- 4 large garlic cloves, minced
- 1¼ cups frozen peas
- 1 can black eyed peas, rinsed well
- 3 to 4 tablespoons extra virgin olive oil
- 1 teaspoon sea salt
- 1 teaspoon ground cumin
- 1 teaspoon black pepper
- 2 tablespoons minced cilantro
- 1 or 2 handfuls of baby spinach

Heat oil in a sauté pan over medium heat. Add onions and sauté on medium-low for 8 to 10 minutes until they start to brown and become very fragrant.

Add garlic and stir around for about 1 minute. Add chorizo meat and keep it moving around with a wooden spoon to break it apart and combine well with onion and garlic.

Allow to cook for about 10 minutes or until the meat is almost completely cooked through. If mixture begins to dry out, you can add some water to keep it from sticking to the pan.

Next, add squash and peas. Stir a few times during the next 3 to 4 minutes to make sure that everything is cooking evenly. You may even want to keep it covered so that you can really utilize the heat here.

Once vegetables are tender, add beans and seasonings. Adjust to your liking; however, keep in mind that the chorizo is generally quite flavorful and salty, so you do not need to add much to the mix.

Add a handful or two of baby spinach and combine with ingredients until wilted.

Serve over brown rice topped with freshly chopped tomato and avocado!

Lasts four days in fridge. Leftovers can be frozen up to three months.

ROASTED BRUSSELS SPROUTS

Vegetarian / Vegan / Paleo / Dairy-free / Egg-free / Nut-free
Serves 4

- 1 bag of Brussels sprouts, rinsed, ends trimmed and cut in half
- 1 large onion, coarsely chopped
- 2 tablespoons extra virgin olive oil
- ½ teaspoon sea salt
- ½ teaspoon black pepper
- ½ teaspoon garlic powder
- Preheat oven to 350°F.

Combine all ingredients in a bowl and toss well to evenly coat the vegetables.

Line a baking sheet with foil or parchment. Add vegetables in a single layer to baking sheet.

Place in oven for 15 minutes, then stir up the vegetables so nothing gets burned.

Return vegetables to the oven for another 10 to 15 minutes depending on how roasted you'd like your sprouts to be.

Lasts up to three days in fridge.

SPICY SWEET POTATO WEDGES

Vegetarian / Vegan / Paleo / Dairy-free / Egg-free / Nut-free
Serves 4

- 2 large sweet potatoes, cut in wedges or matchsticks
- 1 teaspoon cumin
- 1 teaspoon paprika
- 1 teaspoon chili powder
- Sea salt and pepper, to taste
- Dash of cayenne
- 2 tablespoons extra virgin olive oil

Preheat oven to 425°F. In a large mixing bowl combine all ingredients and toss until potatoes are well coated. Lay potatoes in a single layer on a large baking sheet.

Bake for 25 to 30 minutes, turning the potatoes once halfway through cooking (at the 12 to 15 minute mark).

Remove potatoes and serve.

Lasts three days in fridge.

ROASTED BEETS

Vegetarian / Vegan / Paleo / Dairy-free / Egg-free / Nut-free
Serves 4

- 4 fresh large beets
- 1 teaspoon dried thyme
- Extra virgin olive oil
- Sea salt
- Red wine vinegar, to taste (optional)

Preheat oven to 425°F.

Chop off 'tail' and leaf base of the beet. Scrub well under warm water. Wrap each beet in aluminum foil and place each on a baking sheet in the oven for about 40 minutes, or until you see some red juice begin to ooze from the tin-foil ball. Remove from oven, open foil, and let cool, about 5 minutes.

Use a paper towel to pick up each beet one at a time and gently use it to rub the skin off the beet. Cut beets into chunks and place in bowl. Add oil, thyme, and sea salt. Add a splash of red wine vinegar if using.

Must be eaten within two days.

ROASTED CHERRY TOMATOES & BEANS

Vegetarian / Vegan / Dairy-free / Egg-free / Nut-free
Serves 4

- 4 cups cherry tomatoes, halved
- 1 small onion, chopped
- 1 tablespoon fresh rosemary, minced
- 2 medium garlic cloves, minced
- 1 can butter beans, rinsed
- 2 tablespoons extra virgin olive oil
- 1 teaspoon balsamic vinegar
- Sea salt, to taste
- ¼ teaspoon white pepper

Preheat oven to 425°F. Line a baking sheet with foil or parchment. Combine tomatoes, garlic, onion, rosemary, pepper, and olive oil in a bowl. Toss until everything is evenly coated and spread into one layer across baking sheet.

Roast until tomatoes and onions are soft. Remove from oven and combine with beans, vinegar, and salt. Adjust seasonings to taste.

Lasts three days in fridge.

SQUASH & PEAS

*Dairy-free / Egg-free / Nut-free / Vegan option***
Serves 4

- 1 Vidalia onion, diced
- 1 zucchini, chopped
- 1 yellow squash, chopped
- 1 tablespoon minced garlic
- 1½ cups peas, heated up
- 2 to 3 tablespoons extra virgin olive oil** (or other fat like bacon, chicken, etc.)
- Sea salt to taste
- 1/8 teaspoon black pepper
- 3 small dashes of turmeric

Heat oil over medium heat and add onions. After 3 or 4 minutes, add garlic and keep moving for another few minutes.

Add the zucchini and squash and combine well. Cook for another 5 minutes and then add peas and spices.

Toss well and adjust seasonings to taste.

For vegan option, use extra virgin olive oil.

Lasts four days in fridge.

EASY GUACAMOLE

Vegetarian / Vegan / Paleo / Dairy-free / Egg-free / Nut-free
Serves 4

- 2 ripe avocados, cubed
- Juice of 1 lime
- ½ teaspoon garlic powder OR 2 garlic cloves, minced
- Handful chopped fresh cilantro
- ½ teaspoon cumin
- ½ teaspoon pepper
- 1 teaspoon sea salt
- Dash of chili powder
- Tomatoes and red onion, diced (optional)

Scoop flesh of avocado into bowl and gently mash with a fork. Add in remaining ingredients and mix well. Adjust seasonings to taste. To store, place in an airtight container and smooth over the top layer with a spoon so that the surface is flat.

Lasts for two to three days, or until it turns grey. If it darkens on the top within the 'safe to eat period,' but is still fresh underneath, you can scrape off the darkened area and eat the brighter green guacamole.

QUICK APPLE CRISP

Vegetarian / Vegan / Dairy-free option / Egg-free / Nut-free*
Serves 4

- 3 large sweet apples, chopped
- 2 tablespoons extra virgin olive oil* (or butter or ghee)
- A few dashes of sea salt
- 1 teaspoon pumpkin pie spice
- Low-sugar granola
- 2 dashes of cardamom (optional)

Heat oil or butter over medium heat in a sauté pan. Add apples and spices and sauté everything for about 5 minutes or until apples become soft. Adjust seasonings to your taste.

Pour apples into your dish of choice and sprinkle with granola to cover the top evenly when you're ready to eat. Enjoy immediately!

GF SAVVY TIP
You can save the sautéed apples and add them to yogurt or have them as a snack. They reheat well and are very versatile.

Best if eaten immediately after topping with granola.

WINTER RICE PUDDING

Vegan / Vegetarian / Dairy-free / Egg-free
Serves 6

- 1 cup brown rice, already cooked
- 1½ cups almond milk
- 1 large apple, cored and cubed
- ½ cup raisins
- 1/8 cup unsweetened, shredded coconut
- 1 teaspoon cinnamon, ground
- 2 to 3 dashes of nutmeg, ground
- 2 to 3 dashes of cloves, ground
- 4 to 5 dashes of sea salt
- 1 tablespoon organic creamy peanut butter or other nut butter (optional)
- Maple syrup (optional)

Combine almond milk, apple, raisins, coconut, sea salt, cinnamon, nutmeg, and cloves in a pot. Bring to a boil, then turn to low and simmer for 10 minutes.

Mix in brown rice and cook for another few minutes until the mixture thickens. Remove from heat and serve warm or allow to cool to room temperature and serve whenever you're ready for dessert!

If you'd like a nutty flavor, stir in peanut (or other nut) butter. If you're looking for a bit of extra sweetness, use a small amount of maple syrup.

Lasts four days in fridge.

COCONUT WATER FREEZER POPS

Vegan / Vegetarian / Paleo / Dairy-free / Egg-free / Nut-free
Makes 4 popsicles

- 1 cup coconut water
- 1 banana
- 1 cup strawberries, hulled

Combine ingredients in a blender and purée until smooth (or to your desired consistency).

Pour into freezer molds and place in a level area of your freezer until solid.

To remove the popsicles, run your mold under hot tap water until the seal of the frozen liquid releases and you can easily pull each pop out. (If you don't do this, you WILL pull the handle out without the pop.)

GF SAVVY TIP
You can blend in other fruits and also try the various flavors of coconut water out there. The passion fruit coconut water from Vitacoco® is a personal favorite.

CHAPTER 20

RESOURCES

Gluten Free School
www.glutenfreeschool.com

Jennifer's Recommended Products
www.glutenfreeschool.com/resources/store

Triumph Dining Gluten-Free Grocery Guide
www.triumphdining.com

Celia's Marketplace Gluten-Free Grocery Shopping Guide
www.ceceliasmarketplace.com

Dirty Dozen ™ Food List
www.ewg.org/foodnews/summary.php

Amazon
www.amazon.com